ISLAM ADDRESSES
CONTEMPORARY ISSUES

ISLAM

ADDRESSES

CONTEMPORARY ISSUES

Ali Ünal

Light

New Jersey
2006

Published by The Light, Inc.
26 Worlds Fair Dr. Suite C
Somerset, New Jersey, 08873, USA
www.thelightpublishing.com

Library of Congress Cataloging-in-Publication Data
Unal, Ali.
  Islam addresses contemporary issues : Ali Unal.
    p. cm.
  ISBN 0-9704370-3-X
  1. Islam--20th century. 2. Islam--Essence, genius, nature. 3.
  Islam--Appreciation. 4. Islam--Doctrines. I. Title.
  BP163 .U53 2002
  297.2--dc21

                                                        2002001207

Printed by
Sistem Matbaacılık
Istanbul, Turkey
January 2006

TABLE OF CONTENTS

INTRODUCTION

I slam has the dubious distinction of being the most poorly introduced and understood religion, worldview, and lifestyle in the world today. The groundwork for this misunderstanding was laid during the Ottoman State's 300-year decline.[1] After representing Islam almost fully and the Islamic world for centuries, it began to lose military and economic ground to Europe. This was followed by the Muslim intelligentsia's surrender to European currents of thought.

Christianity, generally accepted as one of modern Western civilization's three constituents, historically has been perceived to be at odds with science due to the encounters between the Church and science circles during the Middle Ages. Despite this, the West continues to proclaim its Christian identity, especially when dealing with Islam and the Muslim world. Due to centuries of doctrinal innovations in Christianity and the many subsequent misunderstandings, many in the West have started to view Christianity as a system of dogmatic belief cut off from science and free thought. These minds motivated by materialist thought and Renaissance have asserted that Christianity was unrelated to the mind, free thought, and investigation, and with its Divine origin in doubt.

Thus, over time religion in the West came to be regarded as a product of the human mind by many intellectuals, especially those under the influence of scientific materialism. Anthropologists stated that religion reflects human weakness and vulnerability when confronted with nature and natural forces. Sociologists said it mirrors social life and its values. Psychologists asserted that it reflects our suppressed natural instincts. Such views were adopted by most intellectuals in the Islamic world, who then began to perceive Islam in the same way.

At a time when it is clear that Islam never became lost and has retained its original essence in the Qur'an and the Prophet's Sunna[2] throughout history, a new danger has arisen: The implication that Islam is an ideology of conflict, force, and terror. Unfortunately, those who obscure Islam's true face and beauty, either consciously or unconsciously, have contributed to this new intrigue dished up and served out in the West.

This book, composed of articles and studies written at various times, reveals Islam's true face on several intellectual issues. Within the framework of today's most timely and discussed topics, Islamic and Western conceptions are compared frequently. Islam's perspective is presented, misconceptions regarding Islam are examined, and the relationship between humanity and religion is discussed. Humanity, whose individual members form the subject matter of psychology as well as whose social constructs form the subject matter of sociology, is studied. Modern Western thought concerning humanity's make-up is examined, as is Islam's view of humanity.

This is followed by several controversial subjects: the nature of science, the relationship between religion (particularly Islam) and science, and the breadth and depth of Islam's perspective on science. In conclusion, the West's philosophies of history and Islam's concept of history are analyzed.

Given the above, a degree of repetition is unavoidable. I would like to thank those who have helped me in this endeavor. All footnotes identifying people or explaining concepts are taken from www.britannica.com, unless otherwise indicated.

— Ali Ünal

CHAPTER 1

Preliminary Articles

PRELIMINARY ARTICLES

THINKING STRAIGHT AND HOW TO ACHIEVE IT

Some truths are absolute, universal, and without exception; others are general and even relative. For example, God's Existence with His "Essence," Attributes, Names, and acts are absolute and universal truths, as are the principles of belief.[1] General truths, such as those that can be examined by physics, chemistry, and other sciences, contain exceptions. Relative truths, those showing differences in color, tone, and character, depend on time, individuals, or conditions as opposed to seriousness, discipline, gentleness, and tolerance. Relative truths far outnumber absolute and universal truths.

If we define knowledge as "an accumulation of information obtained as a result of one's effort, merits, and capabilities," then we come to this world knowing nothing and encounter an endless universe in which innumerable creatures come together and countless events unfold. Everything in the universe outside of our influence is in its proper place and characterized by the reign of complete order, harmony, and balance. The spiritual and scientific principles underlying these three unshakable characteristics of this vast and complex universe, of which the human body comprises a miniature, are the sum of truth or truths.

Such sciences as physics, chemistry, and biology, regardless of their accuracy or lack thereof, examine the universe and universal relationships with their specific principles. Scientific, existentialist, and other types of philosophers use the resulting scientific data, while sociologists and psychologists use the human relations. In contrast, Islam and other monotheistic religions (in their original forms) see the universe and humanity as expressions of the same truth in all relationships, principles of life, and particulars of existence. Given this, such Divine Books as the Qur'an are an expression of—in fact comprise—the truth that provides universal order, harmony, and balance (the totality of truth).

Throughout history, the differing views of those philosophers, sociologists, and psychologists who have determined or discovered truths have engendered many schools of thought. In contrast, all Prophets and Divine Revelations have taught the same thing. Thus all principles that bring about all of the events and relationships found in the universe and that provide universal order, harmony, and balance, as well as the Qur'an, are the *truth itself*.[2] Thinking and drawing conclusions according to these principles can be called *thinking straight*.

Main Factors of Thinking Straight

Character and intention: Every person is equipped with many capabilities and, simultaneously, caught in a web of mixed emotions and endless need. Our intelligence surrounds and burdens us with sorrows from the past and anxieties for the future, our conscience reminds us of our human responsibility and the essential purpose of our creation, and our will continuously makes us choose between alternatives. Just as we can place these faculties under the command of truth, we can let them be ruled by personal desire, need, self-interest, and ambition. Our inherited characteristics also play an important role in our thought. The sum of these characteristics is called *nature* or *character*.

People ruled by self-interest, desire, and moral weakness, who have not found the right direction, find thinking straight to be a very difficult undertaking. This is especially true if they are motivated by such lower emotions as jealousy, revenge, hatred, and hostility. Thus one of the most important conditions for thinking straight is following the Qur'an's spiritual and moral training and guidance.

The elements of our character (e.g., desire, inclination, sensibility, and need) always influence our intentions. When intending to reach a personal goal instead of the truth, we may distort data or twist the truth. In order to strive after the truth and think straight, we must have a sound intention based upon a trained and disciplined character.

We are sent to this world with a nature that is ready to—and must—be trained. Once here, we encounter two main resources for filling our transparent and empty mental cups: Divine inspiration and an environment composed of our immediate family circle, sociocultural milieu (including the media), and schooling. From the moment of birth, we naturally fall under the influence of our immediate family and surroundings. In time, this influence causes us to develop our minds' ideas, modes of thought, and patterns of value and understanding. Our teachers change, reinforce, or renew these.

Many divinely inspired thoughts, depending upon our own effort and concentration, come during this process. Like many scientific discoveries, they can come as dreams or inspirations in the heart. Divinely inspired thoughts, even if always essentially true, assume a color and form (like water assuming a bowl's color and shape) according to our mental make-up, spiritual level, and emotional sensitivity. Thus the mental framework shaped by the family, environment, formal or informal training, as well as received perception modes and value patterns, can be used to measure a person.

At every stage in this life-long educational process that develops our mental make-up, we think and evaluate differently. We see changing thoughts and values as the normal consequence of a constantly developing mental make-up. People who think that every stage is the final one, and then promote their thoughts at that stage as absolutely true, are seriously mistaken. Presenting such thoughts as absolute truths, even while still learning and when one's mind contains many false thought patterns and measurements, is harmful, for it prevents them from learning new ideas, avoiding earlier mistakes, reaching the truth, and engaging in future questioning and investigating. Eventually, such an attitude can lead to deviation or turn people into despots "for the sake of knowledge."

The path to thinking straight passes through sound measures and the resulting healthy perspective. This can be achieved by questioning everything, except absolute truths taken from their source, and a subsequent mental and spiritual purification. The mind must be cleared of mistakes and biases, and the heart of sin and lower emotions. Beyond that, signs of enlightenment leading to the truth and to thinking straight should be followed. Unless these stages are traversed and sound measures and a healthy point of view are obtained, no one, regardless of his or her knowledge or actions, can reach the truth.

Accurate knowledge: Next comes accurate knowledge. For those with a healthy intention and perspective, accurate knowledge is the essential material that engenders thinking straight, just as the right amount of the right flour is essential for making bread. Without it, we cannot think straight. The only way around this is Revelation, but that option ended with the revelation of the Qur'an.[3] Divine inspiration can manifest itself only in a very pure heart. Even with inspiration the range is very limited, for most of life's aspects require accurate knowledge.

Escaping the restrictions of time and conditions, and perceiving time and conditions accurately: These two factors are critical, for ignoring them causes us to be crushed. We must think about subject matters or seek truths unbound to time and conditions if we want to think in a holistic, as opposed to a fragmented, manner.

Even while realizing this, we must use time and conditions to our benefit. Just as the number of eternal absolute truths is small, the number of relative truths is great. Thus, especially when searching for relative truths, a most important path to thinking straight is conducting an accurate assessment of the times, conditions, and people involved. In the case of Islam, a religion that addresses every century, level, character, temperament, and condition, we must know fully the different epochs, social levels, characters, and temperaments in order to avoid making mistakes. Otherwise, the door to catastrophe can be opened in the name of Islam and we might be among those mentioned in:

> Say: "Shall We tell you of those who lose most in respect of their deeds? Those whose efforts have been wasted in this life, while they thought that they were acquiring good by their works?" (18:103-4)

Truth and Relativity

Einstein's[4] theory of relativity (1905) dealt a severe blow to the worldview based on Galileo's[5] laws of simple cause and effect physics, which reached its peak in the nineteenth century. Goethe's[6] observation that "people running after an idea fall into more and more error" was demonstrated tellingly, and scientists were obliged to acknowledge the limitations of scientific theories. For example, Masaryk's[7] admission that: "Theories, after nourishing for a while the organs in the body of science, dry up and fall to the ground like leaves" pointed out how difficult it is to maintain constant and permanent success in science.

For centuries, scientists accused religion of being a collection of dogmas and religious people of being dogmatists. However, when classical physics' limitations were revealed, scientists realized that they were guilty of the same charge. In other words, as Russell[8] put it:

> Newton's[9] law reigned for such a long time and explained so many things that no one believed that it would ever need correcting. But eventually it became apparent that correction was needed. Let there be no doubt about it, one day these corrections will need to be corrected.

Science advances, if and when it does, by trial and error. Despite this, Einstein's theory of relativity, which replaced classical Newtonian physics, is treated in many circles as absolute truth.

That it one day will need revision or even give way to a new theory is not mentioned.

It seems that going to extremes while pursuing a single idea is a constant human trait. While each great idea contains a share of truth, it is not the only means or expression of truth. If we think of truth as a light at the center point of a circle or a straight line, we see that the light is reflected ray by ray to an infinite number of points on the circle's circumference or along the straight line. Each point is touched by a ray of the truth, and therefore each can be said to be true. However, only the light of the truth in the center never changes, since it is absolute; all other points are relative. What gives the relative truth its particular dimensions, properties, and relevance is the receiving point's nature, properties, time, and conditions. This is true for both the natural and social sciences, and for such Islamic sciences as *tafsir* (Qur'anic commentary) and *fiqh* (jurisprudence).

Given this, is there a permanent absolute truth? Yes, such a truth does exist, but only in the spiritual dimension of things. In fact, from one view, even those principles related to the spiritual dimension of things contain exceptions, for they are connected to the visible external dimension and thus are only relative truths. When discussing absolute and general laws, even scientists cannot affirm absolutely their own laws, such as cause and effect, and say: "If the universe is in T_1 condition at this moment, it cannot be concluded that a little later it will be in the same condition."

As stated above, the difference between absolute and general principles is seen in the social sciences and even in such Islamic sciences as *tafsir* and *fiqh*. In the Realm of Unity, however, single and indivisible truth opens the door to countless relative truths in this material and quantitative world. For example, the Qur'an mentions good works as being virtues with inherent value. And yet we know that some types of virtues may not be considered virtue under different circumstances and times. For example, an administrator's serious manner may be considered dignified at work but haughty at home. A weak person's self-respect before a strong person is praiseworthy, but undesirable in a strong person before a weak one.

In the same way, what is erroneous for one person can be meritorious for another. Thus we say: "The pious deeds of righteous people are sometimes the mistakes of those near to God." Again, an act that earns a single merit for one person can earn a million merits for another. As long as there is no conflict with the word's literal meaning, its root is studied, and Arabic's grammatical rules as well as Islam's basic principles are not violated, each meaning that any qualified interpreter derives from those Qur'anic verses open to interpretation must be respected.

The most obvious historical manifestation of a general principle's relative truth is seen in the sphere of justice. Absolute justice considers personal and public rights as equal. But there are times when one or even both sets of rights cannot be protected, when the most fundamental rights encompassing both the individual and society are endangered. During those times when individual rights must be sacrificed for the public good, relative justice becomes necessary. Historically, the institution of a hereditary sultanate in the Muslim world arose from the need to establish public and individual security by ending internal clashes and civil wars. In other words, it was demanded by relative justice. Such justice, required by the necessity of compelling circumstances, gains the same authority as absolute justice.

This world contains such a variety and abundance of colors, shapes, properties, times, and conditions that relativism cannot be avoided. Nevertheless, we need some almost-absolute truths to guide our lives. For example, saying that causality has no creative effect in the universe is absolutely true, for everything is in God's hand. We cannot be absolutely certain of what will happen next, and our lives and that of the world actually consist of this moment.

Living this truth consciously, along with believing and surrendering our free will to God, we must admit that causes operate in a relatively (not absolutely) reliable manner in this life. Drawn over absolute reality like a shawl or veil, these causes allow it to assume an appearance of familiarity or habit and thereby make life livable. Eventually, all technology and science are constructed on this veil. In this broad region of human action and observation, Newton's classical physics has precedence over Einstein's relativity physics.

Relativity reminds us of our vulnerability. Those climbing the ladder of Divine Knowledge find that the highest state they can reach through their heart is the station of amazement. As Prophet Muhammad[10] said: "We did not know You as we should, O Known One," and "How could I see Him? What I saw was light."

Similarly, scientists solve one problem only to discover new ones, a process that eventually causes their trust in science's centuries-old foundations to collapse. Just when they "find" the truth, they see everything slip from their grasp. The fact of relativity makes them exclaim: "The only thing I know is that I don't know anything," which then leads them, like moths circling a light, to flap their wings eternally around the light of Divine Knowledge.

Relativity shows that absolute truth lies only in—and can be known directly only by—Revelation. Therefore we have a clear and absolute need for religion and definitive religious principles. As two people cannot agree even on a simple matter, absolute truth can come only from God. Our duty is to organize our life according to the God-given truth at the point of belief. Understanding that we can attain only a partial truth also means that we acknowledge the space separating multiplicity from oneness. Through its pointing to and yearning for the oneness beyond multiplicity, this understanding functions as an important proof of Divine Oneness.

Relativity is an important measure for living peaceably among people, due to the different professions, temperaments, schools, and sects that have arisen in philosophy, teaching methods, and religions. All dispositions, sects, schools, and methods have a portion of the truth, and none are absolutely wrong or false. The important thing is to unite around a common point. When we look to the past and various catastrophes from the perspective of Divine Destiny, and when we look at future responsibilities and Divine orders from the perspective of free will and human responsibility, it is possible to reconcile even proponents of fatalism and free will.

The essential thing is to live believing that absolute truth, when it touches this world and becomes relevant for us, is relative and thus conditioned by the points, circumstances, and conditions of those receiving it. Based on the analogy given above, countless relative truths reflect the absolute truth located at the center point of the circle or the straight line at innumerable other points, according to each one's properties, color, and design. As long as people recognize, acknowledge, and defer to their own distance from the absolute truth and do not transgress their limits, unmanageable conflicts will not arise. But when people lose this sense of proportion and their capacity to know and propose the truth, when they take what is relative for what is absolute, they fall into error with catastrophic results.

THE CONCEPT OF RELIGION IN THE WEST AND ITS CRITICS

Religion comes from either *relegere* ("to read" or "to pursue together," as well as "legible" and "intelligent") or, much more likely and generally accepted, from *relegare* ("to tie back" or "to bind fast"). Hence a religious person used to mean a monk tied by his vows. *Ligament* and *ligature* also come from this root. For Romans, it meant being tied back, staying connected with ancestral customs and beliefs, or a kind of loyalty. For Christians, the word originally meant being tied back or connected to God.

The corresponding Arabic word is *din*, which literally means obedience, being in debt, restoring one's rights, adopting as a habit, forcing, calling to account, managing, rewarding or punishing, serving, lending, and so on. Muslim theologians describe *din* as the set of principles revealed by God through His Prophets and Messengers, and the set that humanity should follow of its own free will to acquire happiness in both worlds.

The concept of religion may be viewed from two perspectives: the human or the Divine. Followers of monotheistic religions take religion to be God-revealed principles, values, and commandments, and so do not refer to humanity when explaining religion's origin. In contrast, modern Western and Westernized people under the influence of scientific materialism say that humanity created religion and then used anthropology, sociology, and psychology to explain it away.

Western Thought Favors Materialism

Unfortunately, the prevailing attitudes among many Westerners and Westernized intellectuals of the East prevent them from considering Islam as a revealed religion. As a result, they usually understand religion in terms of present-day Christianity. The Qur'an affirms that Jesus came to restore the Torah's laws, with the exception of making some unlawful things lawful:

> And (I [Jesus] have come) confirming that which was before me of the Torah, and to make lawful some of that which was forbidden unto you. I come unto you with a sign from your Lord, so keep your duty to God and obey me. (3:50)

The New Testament also states:

> Do not think that I have come to abolish the Law (of Moses [American Bible Society]) and the teachings of the Prophets. I have come not to do abolish them but to fulfill them (Gideons International)—to make their teachings come true (American Bible Society); to complete or perfect them (Bible Society, Turkish edition). (Matthew 5:17)

Despite this, St. Paul[11] promoted his mission by separating Jesus' message from its relationships with and its origins in Judaism's Mosaic law, a procedure akin to separating a person's skin from his or her body. This paved the way for wedding Christianity with Roman laws and rites, focusing on the Kingdom of God in the next world, and relegating nature and this world to a lesser (eventually secular) domain. This is part of the reason why modern Western thought favors materialism and rejects religion's Divine origin.

Western Views of Religion

According to the assumptions of modern Western thought which was shaped in the nineteenth century and affected scientific circles even in the Muslim world during the twentieth, humanity is moving continually and irreversibly toward that which is better. During this "progress," it has passed through certain stages of intellectual and civilizational development. Anthropologists have concentrated on the theory of religion's evolution and reached different conclusions. Frazer[12] sought its origin in magic, Taylor[13] sought it in animism, Schmidt[14] sought it in original monotheism, and others sought it in preanimism, totemism, fetishism, or polytheism. Later anthropologists concentrated on religion's role in society rather than its origin. While social anthropologists considered religion to be part of society and concentrated on field studies of particular tribes or analyses of myth, ritual, and symbol, cultural anthropologists saw it as a set of beliefs, rites, and institutions.

To illustrate the differences of opinion arising among those who, either from ignorance or other limitations, offer their definition of a matter, Rumi[15] made this analogy: "Some blind people encounter an elephant and, after touching different parts of its body, claim that it is a heavy thick column, a hard flexible pipe, and so on." This is what those who try to explain religion's origin have achieved in the West. Just as anthropologists draw different conclusions, sociologists put forward different opinions about religion's origin.

The sociology of religion found its leading analysts in Durkheim and Weber.[16] The former stressed the social functions of religion as a stabilizing factor created by society to express its ideals and to unify itself. Weber, more dynamic and positive, saw religion's Prophetic side as an instrument for shaping and changing society and tried to work out what aspect of Western religious attitudes or culture shaped the formation of capitalism. Other sociologists focused more on particular religious groups and institutions.

The psychology of religion centers upon the individual and his or her religious experience. One main exponent of this was James,[17] who described the religion of the healthy-minded and the sick soul; the religion of the once-born and the twice-born; and the psychological basis of prayer, meditation, mysticism, and conversion. Freud[18] based his research on theories of infantile sexuality and, despite opposition from friends, patients, and medical colleagues, continued to develop them. He emphasized the importance of childhood sexual experiences, regarded religion as necessary illusions (delusions) and projections, and argued that dreams, like neuroses, were disguised manifestations of repressed sexual desires.

More recent work in this field has centered upon how different religious people or institutions are, what mature religious belief is, the spiritual potentialities of human nature, and the stages of religious development in children and adults.

The common denominator in the Western "scientific" analysis of religion is that it is a human invention designed either to project repressed desires or weaknesses or the result of individual or collective efforts to systematize a community's beliefs and rites. The corollary is that as science develops, people will no longer need religion, which Feuerbach[19] wrote is a dogma contradicted by fire and life insurance policies, railways and steamships, modern military and industrial schools, and modern society's theaters and science museums. According to Marx,[20] religion is the opiate of the masses and inevitably will become a thing of the past.

Comte[21] divides human history into three periods: The period of religion, when primitive people feared natural events and forces and needed to believe in a Supreme Being; the period of metaphysics, when humanity reached a higher level of intellectual maturity; and the period of science, when there is no room (or need) for religion because reason and science will solve all human problems. Some people may continue to follow a reduced religion, comprised of basic moral and spiritual principles, in order to satisfy their emotional and spiritual needs and lead an upright life. But religion should not transgress its limits and must not interfere in society's collective—especially political—life. According to Buisson,[22] secularism will not wipe out religion altogether, but will diminish it considerably and destroy the force of its dogmas and the basis of its doctrines.

Before proceeding to criticize Western views of religion, we will summarize other definitions of religion by Western thinkers or philosophers:

Hegel[23] considers religion to be a certain view of the universe. Croce,[24] an Italian follower of Hegel, defines it as an incomplete philosophy. Kant,[25] dealing with religion in terms of social morality, thinks that religion in practice is seeing our responsibilities as Divine ordinances. Schleiermacher[26] sees religion as a feeling or excitement, an emotion or noble sentiment, that is felt for eternity. While rejecting religion's social and political roles, he considers its spirit or essence as an intuitive knowledge of life's highest values and the metaphysical dimension of existence. Ralph Otto, a contemporary theologian, says religion is a mysterious fear combined with awe that causes us to tremble and yet attracts us to itself. Boutroux's definition is: Religion is that belief and feelings demand their right beside the scientific view.

A Criticism

The positivistic view of religion adhered to in the West, and directed by the dogmas of science and technology, is highly questionable. Positivism regards the West's sociological, economic, military, and political levels as the highest level that humanity can attain—a view that even many Western thinkers have criticized severely. In addition to the existential tension and anxiety, Comte's attempt to establish a humanistic religion toward the end of his life, despite his view of religion as being a mode of thinking or belonging to the second (and long past) period of human history, shows that religion cannot be denied or dismissed as an historical artifact.

Also, despite recent advances in science and technology, extreme sexual freedom, high living and education standards, the world is witnessing a growing interest in and turning to religion. New and primitive religions have emerged (e.g., devil worship), and seeking contentment via authentic or false supernormal phenomena (e.g., telepathy, necromancy, sorcery, and fortune-telling) is becoming common. Moreover, as Fromm[27] puts it, we still see the pursuit of security and guarantees for the future through increased association with insurance companies, trade unions, mighty governments, holdings, and pacts. We have seen communism collapse and religion return to those countries formerly under its rule.

Such developments show that the above-mentioned theories of why religion developed are false. These events and trends also demonstrate that Western studies of religion, whether based on sociology, anthropology, or psychology, start from the wrong premises. Religion is a rising value in the world, and more people turn to it every day, whereas modern Western civilization is severely questioned and shows signs of inward decay, even though outwardly it appears to be at the peak of its dominion.

Having lived through the first quarter of the twentieth century, Spengler[28] prophesied the collapse of this civilization with all its skyscrapers, huge metropolises and railways, and foretold that it would become an ethnographic museum. Such "refined" Western intellectuals and scientists as Guénon, Carrel, Planck, Pasternak, and Jeans,[29] have argued that religion will allow humanity to live in another era of happiness. Also, as stated above, the re-emergence of missionary churches in increasing numbers throughout Christendom and the return to Islamic values all over the Muslim world, despite the stern measures taken against Islam by indigenous governments for several decades, demonstrate that it is almost impossible to defeat religion.

RELIGION IN THE QUR'AN

The Qur'an uses *din*, usually translated as "religion," in different contexts with various meanings. The most important and common of these are judging, rewarding, punishing (1:4, 51:6, 82:18-19, 37:53, 56:86); way, law, constitution (12:76); penal law (24:2); the collection of moral, spiritual, and worldly principles, system, and way of conduct (33:5, 40:26); servanthood and obedience (16:52); and peace and order (8:39).

With Islam, God completed the religion He revealed and chose for humanity: *This day I have perfected your religion for you, completed My Favor upon you, and have chosen for you Islam as your religion* (5:3). Literally, Islam means "submission, peace, and salvation." In its most fundamental aspect, Islam is epitomized in the most frequently recited of all Qur'anic phrases, the *Basmala*—In the name of God, the Merciful (*al-Rahman*), the Compassionate (*al-Rahim*). Both words are related to *rahma* (mercy and compassion). God manifests Himself via His absolute, all-inclusive Mercy and Compassion, and Islam is founded upon that affirmation. The Qur'an calls Prophet Muhammad's mission a mercy for all the worlds (21:107).

Islam is distinguished from other religions by several characteristics, among them the following:

Monotheism

Islam is uncompromisingly monotheistic, for its theology begins and ends with God's Unity *(tawhid)*. Given this, the universe is seen as an integral whole of interrelated and cooperative parts in which a splendid coordination, harmony, and order are displayed throughout the universe and within each living organism. This harmony and order come from the Unity of the One Who created them and Who is absolute, without partner, peer, or like. God created, and administers, the universe and everything in it. Natural laws, which we deduce from the universe's operation are, in fact, God's regular ways of creating things and events and administering the universe. Thus the universe, which is governed by and obeys God, is literally *muslim*—submitted to God. This is why its operations are stable, orderly, and harmonious.

Humanity

God created the universe so that He could be known and recognized in all His Names and Attributes. As a result, His creation includes one creature with free will: humanity. Of all creatures, only humanity can manifest the Divine Names the All-Willing, All-Knowing, and All-Speaking. God then endowed us with the knowledge of things [by teaching Adam the "names" of all things] and made us His vicegerent to rule on Earth according to His laws. As having free will means that one must choose, each person's life consists of choosing between right and wrong, good and evil.

God endowed humanity with three principal faculties that are fundamental to our survival and functioning as His vicegerent: an appetite for such things as the opposite sex, offspring, livelihood, and possessions; anger or forcefulness in defense and struggle; and reason or intellect. Since we are tested in this worldly life and are free to choose, God did not restrict these faculties.

According to Islam, our individual and collective happiness lie in disciplining these faculties so that we may produce a harmonious peaceful individual and social life. If they remain undisciplined, immorality, illicit sexual relationships, and prohibited livelihoods, tyranny, injustice, deception, falsehood, and other vices will appear in individuals and throughout society. To prevent the ensuing chaos and suffering, we must submit to an authority that guides and regulates our collective affairs. Since one person will not accept the authority of another, and it is impossible for human intellect to comprehend totally where true human happiness lies in both this and next world, humanity needs a universal intellect, a guidance from beyond human reason and experience to whose authority all may assent freely. That guidance is the religion revealed and perfected by God through His Prophets: Islam.

Prophets

All Prophets came with the same essentials of belief: belief in God's Existence and Unity, the world's final destruction, Resurrection and Judgment, Prophethood and all Prophets without distinction, all Divine Scriptures, angels, and Divine Destiny and Decree (including human free will). They called people to worship the One God, preached and promoted moral virtue, and condemned vice. Differences in particular rules and injunctions were connected with the existing economic and political relationships, for all Prophets before Prophet Muhammad were sent only to their own people and only for their own time. Prophet Muhammad, however, was sent to humanity regardless of time or place. Thus to be a Muslim means believing in all previous Prophets and the original previous Scriptures.

A Prophet, one purified of sin and vice and having a deep relation with God, guides people to truth and sets a perfect example for them to follow. Such people have the following essential characteristics: absolute and complete truthfulness, trustworthiness, communication of the Divine Message; the highest intellectual capacity, wisdom, and profound insight; sinlessness; and no mental or physical defects.[30] Just as the sun attracts planets by the invisible force of gravitation, Prophets attract people by the force of their profound relation with God, certain miracles, and the sheer nobility of their person, purpose, and character.

Belief

Belief, the essence of religion, is far more than a simple affirmation based on imitation. Rather, it has degrees and stages of expansion or development, just as a tree's seed gradually is transformed into a fully grown, fruit-bearing tree. Belief contains so many truths pertaining to God's 1,001 known Names and the realities contained in the universe that the most perfect human science, knowledge, and virtue is belief in and knowledge of God originating in belief based upon argument and investigation. Such belief has as many degrees and grades of manifestation as the number of Divine Names. Those who attain the degree of "certainty of belief coming from direct observation of the truths on which belief is based" can study the universe as a kind of Divine Scripture.

The Qur'an, the universe, and humanity are three manifestations of one truth. In principle, therefore, there can be no contradiction or incompatibility between Qur'anic truths (from the Divine Attribute of Speech) and truths derived from the objective study of its counterpart, the created universe (from the Divine Attributes of Power and Will). An Islamic civilization true to its authentic, original impulse contains no contradiction between science (the objective study of the natural world) and religion (the personal and collective effort to seek God's good pleasure). True belief is not based on blind imitation, but rather appeals to our reason and heart and combines reason's affirmation and the heart's inward experience and submission.

The degree of belief known as "certainty coming from the direct experience of its truths" depends on regular worship and reflection, and those who possess it can challenge the world. Thus the Muslims' foremost duty is to acquire this degree of belief and try, in full sincerity and purely to please God, to communicate it to others. As Said Nursi[31] reminds us:

> Belief in God is creation's highest aim and most sublime result, and humanity's most exalted rank is knowledge of Him. The most radiant happiness and sweetest bounty for jinn and humanity is love of God contained within knowledge of God. The human spirit's purest joy and the human heart's sheerest delight is spiritual ecstasy contained within love of God. All true happiness, pure joy, sweet bounties, and unclouded pleasures are contained within knowledge and love of God.[32]

Worship

Belief engenders different kinds of worship, such as responding to explicit injunctions (e.g., the prescribed prayers, fasting, almsgiving, and pilgrimage) and obeying prohibitions (e.g., avoiding all intoxicants, gambling, usury, killing, oppression, usurpation, and deception,). Those seeking to strengthen their belief and attain higher ranks of perfection should be careful of their heart's and intellect's "acts" (e.g., contemplation, reflection, invocation, recitation of God's Names, self-criticism, perseverance, patience, thankfulness, self-discipline, and perfect reliance upon God). Moral virtues are the fruits of religious life. As Prophet Muhammad said: "I have been sent to perfect virtue."

Collective life

By means of belief and worship, as well as its intellectual, moral, and spiritual principles, Islam educates us in the best possible way. In addition, it uses its socioeconomic principles to establish an ideal society free of dissension, corruption, deception, oppression, anarchy, and terror, one that allows everyone to obtain happiness both in this world and the next.

Many Western intellectuals and their Muslim counterparts assert that serving God or living a religious life is a compensatory device contrived to console people for their own weaknesses and defects. But such people, even though armed with science, technology, and the illusions of freedom from belief and servanthood to a Supreme Being as well as of their own existence as powerful beings, abase themselves before any person or thing, regardless of how low, if they consider it in their self-interest to do so.

People today are stubborn and unyielding, yet degrade themselves for one brief pleasure; unbending, but kiss the feet of devilish people to gain an advantage; conceited and domineering but, since they can find no point of support in their hearts, posture like impotent, vainglorious tyrants; and self-centered egotists who strive to gratify their material, carnal desires and pursue personal or national interests coinciding with their own.

Sincere believers do not degrade themselves. These dignified servants of God reject any worship of all that is not God, even if it is something having the greatest benefit, like Paradise. Though modest and gentle in their nature and bearing, they "lower" themselves voluntarily before others only to the degree that their Creator permits. Though aware of their weakness and neediness before God, they rely upon their One Master's Wealth and Power and so are independent of others.

Modern civilization, especially in its materialistic and colonial aspect, assumes that collective life consists of competing selfish interests that are necessarily in a state of conflict and arbitrated by force or might. To unify its various communities, it promotes an aggressive and negative nationalism that often degenerates into a brutal racism. As a result, most of the world's people have been or remain dominated by this civilization and continue to suffer the accompanying acute misery and humiliation. Meanwhile, the minority that benefits from such a *status quo* gratifies its worldly desires, which are continually stimulated and increased and thereby bring about more competitiveness and anxiety.

The life of religion and serving God accepts right, not force, as the point of support in social life. It proclaims that the aim of individual and collective life is to attain virtue and God's approval instead of realizing selfish interests, and mutual assistance instead of conflict. It seeks the internal and external unity of communities through ties of religion, profession, and country, not through racism and negative nationalism. It works to erect a barrier against worldly desires and encourages us to strive for perfection by urging the soul to pursue sublime goals. Right calls for unity, virtue brings solidarity, and mutual assistance means helping each other. Religion secures brotherhood, sisterhood, and attraction. Self-discipline and urging the soul to virtue bring happiness in this world and the next.[33]

Given all of the above, how did unbelieving modern civilization defeat believing Muslims? According to Said Nursi, Muslims are required to be *muslim* (submitted to God) in all of their attributes and actions, but cannot always be so in practical life. It is the same with non-Muslims, for not all of their attributes and actions necessarily originate in unbelief or transgression. Thus non-

Muslims who acquire *muslim* attributes and conform to Islamic principles can defeat Muslims who neglect to practice Islam.

God has established two kinds of laws: the Shari'a (issuing from His Attribute of Speech and governing our religious life) and the so-called laws of nature (issuing from His Attribute of Will and governing creation and life). The reward/punishment for following/ignoring them is given at different times. Reward and punishment for obeying or disobeying the former usually are given in the next life; for the latter, they are given in this life.

The Qur'an constantly draws our attention to natural phenomena, the subject matter of science, and urges us to study them. In the first 5 centuries of Islam, Muslims united science and religion, intellect and heart, and the material and the spiritual. Later on, however, Europe took the lead in science due to its unconscious obedience to the Divine laws of nature, and thus was able to dominate the Muslim world, which no longer practiced Islam's religious and scientific aspects.

Power and force have some right in life and were created for some wise purpose. Armed with power through science and technology, Europe defeated the Muslim world. Just as a sparrow develops its defensive strengths and skills by defending itself against a hawk's attacks, God allows unbelief to attack Islam so that Muslims will acquire the skills and strengths needed to restore Islam to its original purity and regain its authority in their lives.

THE NECESSITY OF RELIGION[34]

The following allegory explains the world, our spirits within it, and religion's nature and worth. It also explains how the absence of "true religion" makes this world the darkest dungeon and unbelievers the most unfortunate creatures, and why belief in God's Existence and Unity, as well as reliance upon Him, opens the universe's secret sign and saves our souls from darkness.

Two brothers travel together.[35] Coming to a fork in the road, they see a wise old man and ask him which way they should take.

He tells them that the right fork requires observance of the road's law and brings a certain security and happiness, while the left fork promises a certain kind of freedom as well as certain danger and distress. He tells them to choose. The well-disciplined brother, relying on God, takes the right fork and accepts dependence on law and order.

The other brother takes the left fork for the sake of freedom. He seems comfortable, but in fact feels no inner tranquillity. Reaching a desert, he suddenly hears the terrible sound of a beast that is about to attack him. He runs away and, seeing a waterless well 60 meters deep, jumps into it. Halfway down, he grabs a tree growing out of the wall to break his fall. The tree has two roots, both of which are being gnawed away by two rats, one white and the other black. Looking up, he sees the beast waiting for him.

Looking down, he sees a horrible dragon almost at his feet, its large mouth open to receive him. Looking at the wall, he notices that it is covered with laboring insects. Looking again at the tree, he notices that although it is only a fig tree, it miraculously has many different fruits growing on it, such as walnuts and pomegranates.

Hanging in the well, he does not understand what has happened. He cannot imagine that somebody has caused all of these things to happen, for he cannot reason. Although inwardly distressed and despite his spirit's and heart's complaints, his evil-commanding self pretends everything is fine and so ignores their weeping. Pretending that he is enjoying himself in a garden, he starts eating all kinds of fruits—for free. But some of them are poisonous and will harm him.

In a *hadith qudsi*,[36] God says: "I will treat My servants in the way they think of Me." This person sees everything happening to him as unimportant, and thus that is the way it is for him. He neither dies nor lives well, but merely persists in an agony of suspense.

The wiser and well-disciplined brother always thinks of the good, affirms the law, and feels secure and free. Finding beautiful flowers and fruits or ruined and ugly things in a garden, he focuses on what is good and beautiful. His brother cannot, for he has concerned himself with evil and finds no ease in such a garden. The wise brother lives according to: "Look on the good side of everything" and thus is generally happy with everything.

Upon reaching a desert and encountering a beast, he is afraid. But thinking that it must be serving someone, he is not so afraid. He also jumps down a well and, halfway down, catches hold of some tree branches. Noticing two rats gnawing at the tree's two roots, as well as the dragon below and the beast above, he finds himself in a strange situation. But unlike his brother, he infers that everything has been arranged by someone and constitutes a sign.

Thinking that he is being watched and examined, he understands that he is being directed and guided as a test and for a purpose. His curiosity aroused, he asks: "Who wants to make me know him?" Meanwhile, he remains patient and self-disciplined. This curiosity arouses in him a love for the sign's owner, which makes him want to understand the sign, what the events mean, and to acquire good qualities to please its owner.

He realizes that the tree is a fig tree, although it bears many kinds of fruit. He is no longer afraid, for he realizes that it is a sample catalogue of the unseen owner's fruits prepared for guests. Otherwise, one tree would not bear so many different fruits. He starts to pray earnestly and, as a result, the key to the secret is inspired in him. He declares: "O owner of this scene and events, I am in your hands. I take refuge in you and am at your service. I desire your approval and knowledge of you." The wall opens, revealing a door (the dragon's mouth) leading onto a wonderful, pleasant garden. Both the dragon and the beast become two servants inviting him in. The beast changes into a horse upon which he rides.

And so, my lazy soul and imaginary friend! Let's compare their positions and see how good brings good and evil brings evil. The one who took the left road of self-trust and self-willed freedom is about to fall into the dragon's mouth. He is always anxious and lonely, and considers himself a prisoner facing the attacks of wild beasts. He adds to his distress by eating apparently delicious but actually poisonous fruits that are only samples; they are not meant to be eaten for their own sake, but to persuade people to seek and become customers of the originals. He changes his day into darkness. He wrongs himself, changing his situation into a hell-like one, so that he neither deserves pity nor has the right to complain.

In contrast, the one who took the right way is in a fruitful garden and surrounded by servants. He studies every different and beautiful incident in awe, and sees himself as an honored guest enjoying his generous host's beautiful servants. He does not eat up the fig tree's fruits; rather, he samples them and, understanding reality, postpones his pleasure and enjoys the anticipation.

The first person is like one who denies his favored situation in a summer garden surrounded by friends, and instead, becoming drunk, imagines himself among wild beasts in winter and complains thereof. Wronging himself and insulting his friends, he deserves no mercy. The other person, who accepts trustingly what is given and observes the law, sees and accepts reality, which for him is beautiful. Respecting the owner of reality, he deserves mercy. Thus can we attain a partial understanding of: *Whatever good befalls you is from God, and whatever ill befalls you is from yourself* (4:79).

Reflecting upon these two brothers, we see that one's inner self prepared a hell-like situation for him, corresponding to his own attitude of reality, whereas the other's potential goodness, positive intention, and good nature led him to a very favored and happy situation. Now, I say to my own inner self as well as to the reader's: If you desire success, follow the guidance of the Qur'an.

The gist of the allegory is as follows: One brother is a believer; the other is an unbeliever. The right road is that of the Qur'an and belief; the left road is that of unbelief and rebellion. The garden is human society and civilization, which contain both good and evil, cleanliness and pollution. A sensible person "takes what is clear and pleasant, leaves what is turbid and distressing," and proceeds with a tranquil heart. The desert is Earth, the beast is death, the well is our lifetime, and 60 meters is our average lifespan of 60 years.

The tree in the well is life, and the two rats gnawing on its roots are day and night. The dragon is the grave's opening. For a believer, it is no more than a door opening on the Garden. The insects are the troubles we face, and in reality are gentle warnings from God that prevent believers from becoming heedless. The fruits are the bounties of this world presented as samples from the blessings of the Hereafter, inviting customers toward the fruits of Paradise.[37] The sign shows the secret will of God in creating. It is opened with belief, and its key is: "O God, there is no god but God; God, there is no god but He, the Ever-Living, the Self-Subsistent."

For one brother, the dragon's mouth (the grave) changes into a door to the Garden (Paradise). For the other, as for all unbelievers, the grave is the door to a place of trouble (Hell). The beast changes into an obedient servant, a disciplined and trained horse. In other words, for unbelievers death is a painful detachment from loved ones, an imprisonment after leaving the Paradise-like Earth. For believers, it is a means of reunion with dead friends and companions. It is like going to their eternal home of happiness, a formal invitation to pass into the eternal gardens, an occasion to receive the wage bestowed by the Most Compassionate and Merciful One's generosity for services rendered to Him, and a kind of retirement from the burden of life.

In sum, those who pursue this transient life place themselves in Hell, even though they stay in what appears—to them—as a paradise on Earth. Those who seek the eternal life find peace and happiness in both worlds. Despite all troubles, they thank God and patiently conclude that all of this is merely a waiting room opening onto Heaven.

THE ISLAMIC VIEW OF HUMANITY

Immediately after our birth, we have no conscious knowledge of ourselves or our surrounding environment. And yet we are not aliens, but rather beings who are fitted to survive here. For example, each person's body is made up of the same elements that exist in nature. The building blocks making up Earth's mineral, vegetable, and animal elements also constitute the sperm and the egg that, when joined, initiate our earthly life. And yet no one knows how this inanimate matter is transformed into living forms. We can say only that it is a direct gift of the Creator. Thus we are children of nature and aware of ourselves as creatures made by the Creator. Such awareness makes us aware of the second aspect of our being: our heavenly aspect.

Typically, children are born into a welcoming environment and know the embrace of parents and a wider family of relatives. Moreover, they are immediately provided with the most perfect nourishment: a mother's milk. As they grow, children experience the world as a fully ordered environment of sight and sounds, heat and light and rainfall, and an infinite diversity of plants, fruits, and animals. All of these enable children to exercise and enlarge the senses, feelings, and intellect implanted within them by the Creator.

Likewise, their bodies function without their conscious effort or decision. Each person receives a minutely arranged and coordinated physical body as a gift from the Creator when He bestows life, so that that life may be supported and mature. Very little of what we have can be said to be our own doing. In fact, without the Creator's help, we could not even manage our own bodies and therefore would die.

The One Who created the universe and subjected it to our stewardship is also the One Who created us. Given this, it makes perfect sense to consider what our responsibility is and, realizing all that we have been given, to reflect upon how we will answer for ourselves and for what has been placed in our care. Human responsibility before the Creator is voluntary, whereas all non-human creatures perform their duties without reflection but also without defect.

The apparent efficiency of modern technology obscures our relative impotence and vulnerability. We cannot create even a leaf or a fly, although we are free to tamper with God's creation to the extent that He wills. We have no dominion over our body's operations, such as its hunger or thirst, or the world. We cannot determine our parents, our time and place of birth and death, or our physique or physical structure. We have to use the natural world to sustain and enlarge our lives.

The One Who subjected nature to us also implanted within us the necessary intellectual faculties by which we can use nature. Our intellect is capable of obtaining some knowledge of nature's orderly operations and then formulating laws based upon the observed uniformity and reliability. These laws are our imperfect human intimations of the ways God creates things and events and manages or control them.

Humanity and Development

The quality of being human comes from our immaterial and spiritual aspects, not from our natural and material aspects. The spirit and intellect do not originate in the physical body, for the spirit's departure from a dead body reduces that body to something that will decompose into the soil. The body remains for a while, but all of its former senses are now absent. This means that the spirit uses the body, and that only life gives the body any meaning.

This body–spirit relation can be understood better by the following analogy: A factory, no matter how complex, sophisticated, and excellent, has no more value than a pile of mechanical junk if there is no electricity to operate it. This does not mean that the spirit is everything in and of itself and that the body is junk; rather, the spirit needs matter or a corporeal form to express its powers and functions.

A fruit tree's future life is encapsulated in its seed, and a tree is worth only as much as the value of the fruit it yields. In the same way, each person's life-history is recorded and is of value only in proportion to the number of good deeds done and the level of virtue attained. Again, just as a tree increases by means of the seeds in its fruit, we prosper by our good deeds, the weight and consequence of which will be revealed to us in the future.

We scatter our deeds in this world and harvest the results in the next world. Given this, the All-Majestic, All-Powerful, All-Wise Creator, Who brings us into existence from non-existence and Who brings us to life by breathing the spirit into our bodies (fashioned from elements in nature), will resurrect us after we decompose into the ground. For Him, doing so is as easy as bringing day after night, spring after winter, and making what appears to be dry wood at the end of autumn yield grapes the following summer.

In addition, we have three principal drives: desire, anger, and intellect. We desire or lust after the opposite sex and love our children and worldly possessions. We direct our anger at what stands in our way and defend ourselves by using it. Our intellect enables us to make the right decisions. The Creator does not restrain these drives, but rather requires us to strive for perfection through self-discipline so that we do not misuse them. It is this struggle that determines our humanity, for without it we would have no purpose and would be the same as all other non-human creatures.

Only people mature spiritually and intellectually, for no other part of creation has the necessary ingredient for this process: free will. All of them live lives that are wholly determined within nature, for without free will they have no way to keep themselves within the correct limits. If we ignore these limits, we may usurp the property of others, seek illicit sexual relations, or use our intellect to deceive others.

This is why our powers must be held in check. Our intellect was given to us to be used with wisdom, and our desire and anger were given to us to that we could use them lawfully and in moderation. Moreover, as social beings we must restrain our-selves so that wrongdoing, injustice, exploitation, disorder, and revolts do not occur.

But what is lawful and right, moderate and wise? Who decides the criteria, and how will they be accepted by people? Who am I? Where do I come from? What is my final destination? What does death demand from me? Who is my guide on this journey, beginning from clay and passing through the stages of a sperm-drop, a blood-clot, and a lump of flesh, another creation where the spirit is breathed into my body, and finally reaching the grave and through there to the Hereafter? In all of these ques-tions lies the essential problem of human life.

What is Truth?

It is rare for even two or three people to agree on the truth of a matter. If the rich and powerful define truth, their truth will exclude or disadvantage the poor and vice versa. Truth cannot be decided by majority vote, for truth is truth regardless of how many people vote for it. Truth is—and can be determined only by—the Truth, another name for God, Who created humanity and the uni-verse. Our task is to discover that truth and abide by it.

Of course there are some universal truths, such as honesty, generosity, altruism, truthfulness, helpfulness, and compassion. These are essentially reflections of our true nature. Created by the One, Who is All-Wise, All-Generous, and All-Compassionate, every person has an innate inclination toward these virtues. Therefore they are confirmed and established by Islam, which was revealed by God through His Prophets to show humanity how to resolve all of its psychological and social problems.

While constant change is observed in nature, there is an underlying aspect of permanence in everything. For instance, a seed germinates underground and grows into a tree without the laws of germination and growth changing. Likewise the essen-tial purposes and needs of all people, regardless of any external material or other changes in their lifestyles, as well as their impact on our lives and environment, have remained unchanged since the creation of Adam and Eve. All of us share certain general conditions of life and value. For example, we are born, mature, marry, have children, and die; we have some degree of will and common desires; and we share certain values, such as honesty, kindness, justice, and courage.

Thus all Prophets sent by God were sent with the same message of His Absolute Oneness and Absolute Transcendence: He does not beget nor is He begotten, for He is Eternally Self-Existent. Each created being naturally depends on his or her Creator. Only the Creator is Self-Existent, unique, single, non-composite, immune to change, and uncontained by time and space. Belief in such a Divine Being constitutes the primary foundation of Islam, the Divine religion preached by all Prophets. Its other pillars are belief in the Resurrection, all Prophets without distinction, angels, Divine Scriptures, and Divine Destiny (including human free will).

Through sincere belief and worship, as well as adherence to the Prophets' pristine teachings, we can attain the highest degree of elevation—even become worthy of Heaven. There is no other escape from the snares of worldly life, the oppressive ignorance of false human-made systems, or the tyranny of self-appointed priestly authority.

Those who do not use their free will to discipline themselves face the danger of being enslaved by their passions. Such a lack of self-discipline causes us to wrong others, for the goal of such behavior is to satisfy our desires. Since the Divine religion does not allow such wrongdoing, those who pursue it try to corrupt the religion in order to justify their whims and fancies. This causes disorder, oppression, unending conflict, and destruction. God wills mercy for His creation, not oppression or injustice, and that they live in peace so that justice prevails. However, history relates that the followers of all earlier Prophets split into opposing factions and tampered with the religion usually to serve their own interests.

For example, we see this with the Israelites, for over time they broke with the original Torah to a certain extent and finally were enslaved by their materialistic desires. When Jesus was sent to them to restore the Divine religion, little of Moses' pure teaching remained. After the first generation, the followers of Jesus also split into many factions. At one time, there were as many as 300 Gospels. One faction allied itself to the Roman Empire and more or less managed to prevail over the others.

The Nicean Council (325) imposed Christianity throughout the Empire, and eventually a canon of accepted texts emerged as a new Scripture.[38] Christians deified Jesus and the Holy Spirit, thus introducing a mysterious Trinity into the pure teachings of Jesus. Some went beyond this and deified his mother Mary. These dogmas gradually were combined with such other beliefs as blood atonement and Original Sin.[39]

Islam as the Consummation of All Previous Authentic Beliefs

All Prophets before Prophet Muhammad were sent to restore the Divine religion to its original purity by purging all innovations and deviations. This is why Prophet Muhammad was sent after Jesus to preach the same pillars of belief. God revealed to him the Qur'an, which contains the eternal principles for our individual and collective life. Since God decrees that the Qur'an is absolutely and permanently preserved, Prophet Muhammad is the last Messenger.

Unlike any other religion, Islam honors the religious experience of those who came before its revelation, because Islam confirms and completes what is true in those religions. Given this, Muslims say that Prophet Abraham and all other Prophets were *muslim*—totally submitted to God. Such an outlook explains why Islamic civilization, from its very beginnings, was and remains tolerant, plural, and inclusive. It has always been this way, except for the rarest of exceptions.

THE MESSIANIC MISSION ATTRIBUTED TO JESUS TOWARD THE END OF TIME

Humanity and Religion

Some of the first converts to Islam were subjected to severe persecution in Makka. They bore them patiently and never thought of retaliation, as the Qur'an ordered Prophet Muhammad to call unbelievers to the way of God with wisdom and fair preaching, advised him to repel evil with what was better, and to respond to his enemies' sins and faults with forbearance and forgiveness. Makkan intolerance eventually compelled the local Muslims to abandon their homes and property and emigrate to Madina, where they could live according to their beliefs and where Islam's full social and legal dimensions could evolve in peace.

But the Makkans' hostility continued, and in Madina the Muslims became targets of new conspiracies. Although the native Madinan believers (al-Ansar) willingly shared everything with the Emigrants, all suffered privations. In such strained circumstances, God Almighty allowed them to fight their enemies, for they had been wronged and driven from their homes unjustly (22:39).

The Battle of Badr was the first major confrontation of the Muslims and the enemy forces.[40] Although outnumbered, the believers won a great victory. If we do not accept the opinions of some Qur'anic interpreters that *Sura Muhammad*, which contains regulations on how to treat prisoners of war, was revealed before *Surat al-Anfal*, no Divine commandment had been revealed about how captives should be treated. The Muslims did not even know whether they should kill the enemy on the battlefield or take them as prisoners. After the battle, the Prophet consulted, as he always did where there was no specific Divine commandment, with his Companions[41] on this issue.

Abu Bakr[42] said: "O God's Messenger, they are your people. Even though they did you and the believers great wrong, you will win their hearts and cause their guidance if you forgive them and please them." But 'Umar[43] said: "O God's Messenger, they are the leading figures of Makka. If we kill them, unbelief will no longer be able to recover to oppose us. So give to each Muslim his closest kin. Hand 'Aqil over to his brother 'Ali to kill. And his son, 'Abd al-Rahman, to Abu Bakr, and ....[so on]."

God's Messenger turned to Abu Bakr and said:

> "O Abu Bakr, you are like Prophet Abraham, who said: *He who follows me is of me, and he who disobeys me—but You are indeed Oft-Forgiving, Most Compassionate* (14:36). You are also like Jesus, who said: *If You punish them, they are Your servants. If You forgive them, You are the All-Mighty, the All-Wise* (5:118).

Then he turned to 'Umar and said:

> "O 'Umar, you are like Noah, who said: *O my Lord! Leave not even a single unbeliever on Earth!* (71:26). You are also like Moses, who said (of Pharaoh and his chieftains): *Our Lord, destroy their riches and harden their hearts so that they will not believe until they see the painful chastisement.* (10:88)

* * *

The above episode illustrates an important aspect of humanity's nature in relation to the mission of Prophethood and religion in human life.

A person is a "tripartite" being composed of the spirit, the carnal soul, and the body. These three elements are so closely inter-related that neglecting one results in failure to achieve perfection. Given this, each person has been endowed with three essential faculties: spiritual intellect, reason, and will. While alive, each person experiences a continual inner struggle between good and evil, right and wrong. The motor of this struggle is the will, as directed by reason. However, as human reason can be swayed by carnal desires, personal feelings, interests and such emotions as anger and rancor, it needs the spiritual intellect—the source of moral values and virtues—to serve as its guide.

Historically, the Divinely revealed religions have determined what is right and wrong on the authority of their Revealer (God) and of the character of the Prophets who conveyed the Revelation.

Due to their worldly natures, people can become obedient servants of their lust. When such enslaved people gain enough power to rule their fellows, they light fires of oppression and reduce the poor and weak to slaves or servants. Human history is full of such instances. However, as God is All-Just and never approves of oppression, He sent His Prophets in certain eras to guide and correct humanity's individual and collective life.

All Prophets came with the same doctrine, the fundamentals of which are believing in One God, Prophethood, the Resurrection, angels, Divine Scriptures and Divine Destiny (including human free will), and worshipping God. They also conveyed the same moral principles. In this sense, all Divine religions are one and the same. However, the flow of history through epochs varying in cultural, geographical, and socioeconomic conditions required that different Prophets be sent to each nation and that certain differences be made in the acts and forms of worship and the subdivisions of the law—until these conditions allowed Prophet Muhammad to be sent and the religion to be completed. After this, in its essentials, religion sufficed to solve all the problems that humanity will encounter until the end of time and is applicable in all conditions.[44]

Moses, Jesus, and Muhammad

Islam, as the last, universal form of the Divine religion, orders its followers to believe in all of the Prophets. Thus being a Muslim also means being a follower of Jesus, Moses, and all other Prophets.

The Qur'an declares:

> The Messenger believes in what has been revealed to him by his Lord, and so do the believers. They all believe in God and His angels, His Scriptures, and His Messengers: *"We make no distinction between any of His Messengers"*—and they say: *"We hear*

and obey. Grant us Your forgiveness, our Lord. To You is the jour-neying." (2:285)

As historical conditions required that the messages of all previous Prophets be restricted to a certain people and period, certain principles were stressed in those messages. Also, God bestowed special favors on each Prophet and community according to the dictates of the time.

For example, Adam was favored with knowledge of the Names, the keys to all branches of knowledge; Noah was endowed with steadfastness and perseverance; Abraham was honored with intimate friendship with God and being the father of numerous Prophets; Moses was given the ability to administer and was exalted by being God's direct addressee; and Jesus was distinguished with patience, tolerance, and compassion. All Prophets have some share in the praiseworthy qualities mentioned, but each one surpasses, on account of his mission, the others in one or more of those qualities.

When Moses was raised as a Prophet, the Israelites were leading a wretched existence under the Egyptian Pharaohs. Due to the Pharaohs' despotic rule and oppression, slavery had become ingrained in the Israelites' souls and was now part of their character. To reform them, to equip them with such lofty feelings and values as freedom and independence, and to rebuild their character and thereby free them from subservience to the Pharaohs, Moses came with a message containing stern and rigid rules. This is why the Book given to him was called Torah (Law). Given that his mission required that he be a somewhat stern and unyielding reformer and educator, it was natural for him to pray in reference to Pharaoh and his chieftains: *Our Lord, destroy their riches and harden their hearts so that they will not believe until they see the painful chastisement* (10:88).

Jesus came at a time when the Israelites had abandoned themselves to worldly pleasure and led a materialistic life. In the Qur'an, we read that:

> O you who believe! Many priests and anchorites in falsehood
> devour the wealth of people and hinder (them) from the Way
> of God. And there are those who hoard gold and silver and
> spend it not in the Way of God. Announce to them a most
> grievous chastisement. (9:34)

and that these same people exploited religion for worldly advantage:

> You see many of them vying in sin and enmity and how they
> consume what is unlawful. Evil is the thing they have been
> doing. Why do the masters and rabbis not forbid them to utter
> sin and to consume the unlawful? Evil is the thing they have
> been doing. (5:62-63)

The Gospels relate a similar sentiment attributed to Jesus:

> You snakes, how can you say good things when you are evil, for
> the mouth speaks of what has filled the heart. A good person
> brings good things out of his or her treasure of good things; a
> bad person brings bad things out of his or her treasure of bad
> things. (Matthew 12:34-35)

> Take care! Be on your guard against the yeast of the Pharisees
> and Sadducees. The teachers of the law and the Pharisees are
> the authorized interpreters of Moses' Law. So you must obey
> and follow everything they tell you to do. Do not, however,
> imitate their actions, because they do not practice what they
> preach. They tie onto people's backs loads that are heavy and
> hard to carry, yet they are not willing to lift even a finger to help
> them carry those loads. They do everything so that people will
> see them ... They love the best places at feasts and the reserved
> seats in the synagogues. They love to be greeted with respect in
> the marketplaces and to have people call them "Teacher" . . .
> How terrible for you, teachers of the Law and the Pharisees.
> You hypocrites ... You give to God one-tenth of the seasoning
> herbs, such as mint, dill, and cumin, but neglect to obey the
> really important teachings of the Law, such as justice, mercy,
> and honesty. You should practice these without neglecting the
> others. (Matthew 23:1-7, 22)

When Jesus was sent to the Israelites, the spirit of the True Religion had dwindled away and the religion itself had been reduced to a device for its exponents to rob the common people. So before proceeding to put the Law into effect, Jesus concentrated on belief, justice, mercy, humility, peace, love, repentance for one's sins, seeking God's forgiveness, helping others, purity of heart and intention, and sincerity:

> Happy are those who know they are spiritually poor, for the kingdom of heaven belongs to them. Happy are those who mourn, for God will comfort them. Happy are those who are humble, for they will receive what God promised. Happy are those whose greatest desire is to do what God requires, for God will satisfy them fully. Happy are those who are merciful to others, for God will be merciful to them. Happy are the poor in heart, for they will see God. (Matthew 5:3-8)

As for Prophet Muhammad, he has all of the qualities mentioned above, except that of being the father of Prophets. In addition, because of his mission's universality he is like Moses (he is a warner, established a Law, and fought his enemies) and Jesus (a bringer of good news who preached mercy, forgiveness, helping others, altruism, humility, sincerity, purity of intention, and moral values of the highest degree). Remember that the Qur'an declares that God sent Prophet Muhammad as a mercy for all of creation.

Islam presents God, before all other Attributes and Names, as the All-Merciful and All-Compassionate. By doing this, it indicates that He mainly manifests Himself as the All-Merciful and All-Compassionate, and that His wrath and punishment are shown when attracted by the individual's own unforgivable sins and wrongdoing. But God, the All-Forgiving, forgives most of His servants' sins: *Whatever misfortune befalls you is for what your own hands have earned, and for many (of them) He grants forgiveness* (42:30).

Prophet Muhammad had the mission of both Moses and Jesus. The historical episode mentioned at the article's beginning shows that Abu Bakr mainly represented the mission of

Jesus and that 'Umar mainly represented the mission of Moses. Since Islam must prevail until the end of time, there may be occasions when its followers are required to act, according to circumstances, sometimes as Moses and sometimes as Jesus.

Messianic Mission of Jesus toward the End of Time

The reliable Books of Tradition[45] contain many sayings of Prophet Muhammad that Jesus will return to this world before the end of time and observe Islamic law. Although such Traditions have been interpreted in different ways, they can be interpreted as meaning that, before the end of time, Islam must manifest itself mostly in the dimension represented by Jesus. In other words, the main aspects of his prophethood must be given prominence in preaching Islam. These aspects are the following:

Jesus always traveled. He never stayed in one place, but preached his message on the move. Those who preach Islam must travel or emigrate.

> They must be the repenters, worshippers, travelers (in devotion to the cause of Islam and to convey it), those who bow and prostrate (to God only), command good and forbid evil, and observe God's limits. For them there is good news. (Tawba, 9:112)

Mercy, love, and forgiveness had the first place. Jesus brought good news. Therefore, those who dedicate themselves to the cause of Islam must emphasize these characteristics and, never forgetting that Prophet Muhammad was sent as a mercy for all the worlds and the whole of existence, must convey good news to every place and call people to the way of God with wisdom and fair exhortation. They must never repel others.

The world today needs peace more than at any time in history. Most of our problems arise from excessive worldliness, scientific materialism, and the ruthless exploitation of nature. Everyone talks so much about the danger of war and environmental pollution that *peace* and *ecology* are the most fashionable words on people's tongues. But the same people wish to remove those problems through the further conquest and domination of nature.

The problem lies in rebelling against heaven and in destroying the equilibrium between humanity and nature. This condition is a result of modern materialism's conception of and corrupt attitude toward humanity and nature. Most people are reluctant to perceive that peace within human societies and with nature is possible only through peace with the spiritual order. To be at peace with Earth, one must be at peace with the spiritual dimension of one's existence. This is possible only by being at peace with heaven.

In the Qur'an, Jesus introduces himself as follows:

> I am indeed a servant of God ... He has commanded me to pray and give alms as long as 1 live. He has made me dutiful to my mother, and has not made me oppressive, wicked. (79:31-32)

From the viewpoint of Jesus' promised messianic mission, this means that children will not obey their parents. Thus those who spread Islam in our age must strive to show due respect to their parents and elders, in addition to performing their prayers correctly and helping the poor and needy. The Qur'an enjoins:

> Your Lord has decreed that you worship none but Him, and that you show kindness to your parents. If either or both of them attain old age with you, (show no sign of impatience, and) do not even say "uff" to them, nor rebuke them, but speak kind words to them. (17:23)

One of Jesus' miracles was healing the sick and reviving the dead with God's permission. In other words, respect for life was very important in his message. The Qur'an attaches the same degree of importance to life: *One who kills another wrongly is regarded as having killed humanity; one who saves a life is regarded as having saved humanity* (5:32). Those dedicated to the cause of Islam must attach the utmost importance to life and try to prevent wars, find cures for illnesses, and know that reviving a person spiritually is more important than healing diseases. The Qur'an declares: *O you who believe! Respond to God and the Messenger, when the Messenger calls you to that which will give you life* (8:24).

KILLING FOR RELIGION?

Our consciousness is manipulated and entrapped, to a certain extent, by slogans. Such conceptions as democracy, freedom, and human rights are the three most effective slogans used to benumb public opinion and maintain the world's order. As ideas, even as values, we do not necessarily object to them; rather, we do not approve of them when they are used by certain powers as cynical deceptions that are as corrosive as chemical weapons.

The world powers usually accept tyrannies for as long as they can manipulate them easily. They seek stability in those areas of a country's life that allow their economic interests to function and flourish unopposed. But yet they oppose any democratic country that jeopardizes their interests by seeking political or cultural independence. They interfere in such countries' internal affairs, on the grounds of "democracy and freedom," even though their own human rights' record is by no means good.

Leaving aside colonialism's past and present excesses in different guises, we note the continued existence of racial, cultural, and religious discrimination within their own lands. Concessions are made regularly to extremist political parties (ostensibly to prevent greater popularity); the number of crimes and prisoners continues to increase; and physical torture, especially of activists on behalf of minority interests, is unofficially tolerated. Yet they still claim the right to champion democracy, freedom, and human rights wherever they want to—just as long as it serves their own interests and they can justify the use of military or economic force to their own people.

They wage war thousands of miles away to assert their interests in an island, yet do not allow others the same right in an island on their very borders. Intelligence activities abroad are "heroic" when used by the world powers, but somehow become "barbaric" or "terrorist" when used by other countries seeking to maintain or assert their independence and self-defense. In short, the moral or philosophical value of democracy, freedom, and human rights is utterly compromised by the naked cynicism used to secure their dominion. Such practices remind us of the famous chant in Orwell's *Animal Farm*: "All animals are equal, but some are more equal than others."[46]

Nothing is so effective against such cynicism as serious and sincere religious belief that can inspire the thoughts and actions that govern life. Therefore it is no surprise that political opinion-formers sometimes take swipes at religion on the absurd claim that religion inspires killing. *Time* magazine once presented the Divinely inspired religion—whether Judaism, Christianity, or Islam—as a way of life that encourages "killing for God."[47]

Some extremist groups misrepresent religion as a narrow political ideology and use it to display their hard-heartedness or rigidity, or to sublimate their inferiority or superiority complexes. However, a system that condemns such actions cannot itself be condemned whenever self-professed adherents use it to justify their reprehensible actions.

Religion is a contract between God and humanity, and all of its conditions favor and benefit us. As complex and civilized beings who, in addition to many other things, need a secure coexistence with other people, we seek peace and justice in our individual and collective lives. Just as individual motives differ, humanity's "collective reason" cannot comprehend the true nature of that necessary peace and justice or how to realize it in practice. The subsequent need for a transcendent intellect—religion—therefore was given to us by God. Religion is nothing more than an assemblage of the principles laid down by God for human happiness and security in both worlds and for the realization of justice in practical life.

Since people's essential nature and needs never change over the course of time, all Prophets preached the same fundamentals of religion. Any differences were confined to secondary matters related to the ever-changing circumstances of life. The religion chosen by God Almighty to ensure individual and collective human felicity in both worlds, and which He revealed through all Prophets, is Islam.

Islam means belief in and submission to God, and thereby peace and justice in our individual and collective lives. *Judaism* and *Christianity* are names given to the earlier revelations of Islam under Prophets Moses and Jesus, respectively. No Israelite Prophet ever said *Judaism*. Jesus never claimed to establish *Christianity* on Earth or called himself a *Christian*. *Christian* appears only three times in the New Testament and first by pagans and Jews in Antioch about 43 AD, long after Jesus had left this Earth (Acts 11:26).

Islam can be best summed up in the *Basmala*, the formula that is at the beginning of every Qur'anic chapter and uttered at the start of every good act: In the Name of God, the All-Merciful, the All-Compassionate. The word translated as the All-Merciful is *al-Rahman*, which denotes God as the One Who, out of His infinite Mercy, protects and sustains, as well as guarantees the life of and provides for, *all members of creation without exception.* The word translated as the All-Compassionate is *al-Rahim*, which denotes God as the One Who has special mercy for His good, believing, devoted, and upright servants in both worlds. Moreover, the Qur'an states that the Prophet was *sent as a mercy for all worlds [all species of beings]* (21:107). A religion so based on mercy and compassion seeks to revive, not to kill.

Unfortunately, modern materialistic thought is fed by modern science's extreme positivism and rationalism. It therefore reduces life to the physical or material dimension and ignores the fact that peace, harmony, and contentment in this world depends upon human spirituality. A true spiritual life, one based on enlightening the mind or intellect through scientific knowledge and enlightening the heart and refining feelings through belief, religious knowledge, worship, and inspiration, is essential to the Prophets' preaching. For example, the Qur'an proclaims: *Respond to God and the Messenger, when the Messenger calls you to that which will give you life [which will revive you intellectually and spiritually]* (8:24).

Muhammad Asad, a Jewish convert to Islam, likens Islam to a perfect work of architecture: All its parts are harmoniously conceived to complement and support each other, nothing lacking, with the result of an absolute balance and solid composure.[48] Therefore, it gives almost as much importance to our physical life as it does to our spiritual life. Islam regards each person as the representative of its kind and as having the same value as all humanity.

This is why God condemned Cain (Adam's son), for his unjust murder of his brother Abel introduced murder into history. As a result, he is held indirectly responsible for all killings until the end of time. As this sin is considered so grave, the Qur'an declares that one who kills someone unjustly is just like one who kills all of humanity, and that one who either revives someone either spiritually or physically is just like one who restores all of humanity to life either spiritually or physically (5:32).

Clearly, a religion that attaches such importance to the life of each person will never preach killing for its own sake or glorify it. Islam also does not approve of forced conversion, but rather seeks to remove whatever prevents us from making a free choice of what we will believe by establishing an environment in which freedom of belief and thought is secured. Once this is guaranteed, Islam asks us to use our God-given free will to choose and reminds us that we will be held responsible for it, as well as for whatever we did in this world, in the Hereafter: *There is no compulsion in religion, as right and guidance have been distinguished from wrong and deviation* (2:256).

Prophet Muhammad was attacked many times by his enemies, and sometimes was forced to wage war on them. In all these wars, only about 700 people were killed on both sides. As for modern civilization, we only want to mention some facts to clarify the point: Islam has never had the least part in tens of millions of deaths in the communist revolutions, the suppression of freedom movements in several parts of the world at the cost of millions of lives, and in the adventures in several poor countries, costing more than millions of lives during the wars and many more indirectly since. It is not Islam which caused the death of more than 70 million people, mainly civilians, and forced countless millions more to remain homeless, widowed and orphaned, during and after the two world wars. It is not Islam which gave rise to totalitarian regimes such as Communism, Fascism, and Nazism, and raised war-mongers like Hitler, Stalin, and Mussolini. Islam is not responsible for using scientific knowledge to make nuclear and other weapons of mass destruction. Islam was not responsible for the extermination of tens of millions of natives in many parts of the world, for worldwide colonialism which lasted centuries, and for the slave trade, which costed the lives of tens of millions of people. It is not Islam, nor Muslim peoples even, that are responsible for the establishment of the despotic governments that rule over some Muslim countries and for their oppression, injustice, and bloody regimes. Nor is it Islam which is responsible for modern terrorism, mafia organizations, and for the world-wide smuggling of weapons and drugs.

Did religion or modern civilization, extolled as the most advanced and humane in history, cause the death of more than 60 million people, the majority of them civilians, and force countless millions more to remain homeless, widowed and orphaned, during and after the two World Wars? Is religion responsible for using scientific knowledge to make nuclear and other weapons of mass destruction with which to intimidate poor and weak nations?

If the world powers that want to impose their world order in the name of "world peace, democracy, and human freedom," but in reality for their own political and economic advantage, give themselves the right to commit such atrocities, surely people claiming to serve God can use the same rationale to clear the world of such atrocities and establish true peace and realize true freedom. But believers do not justify, like modern political cynicism does, such atrocities and war-mongering in the name of merely political ends. Believers, unlike unbelievers, realize that those actions sincerely undertaken only in the Name of God, the All-Merciful and the All-Compassionate, and that have no other motive and do not transgress God's limits, can revive truly humane values.

'Ali ibn Abi Talib[49] presents such an example. During a battle, this noble Companion and future caliph, felled his enemy and was on the point of killing him. But at that very moment, the man spat in 'Ali's face. To his surprise, 'Ali released him immediately. Later on he explained his action: The man's action had made him suddenly angry and, therefore, fearing that he would kill the man because of a selfish motive, he released him. This enemy soldier embraced Islam and thus was revived both spiritually and physically.

CHAPTER 2

Islam and Science

ISLAM AND SCIENCE

THE WESTERN CONCEPT OF SCIENCE AND
THE QUR'ANIC APPROACH

Science regards facts as scientific only if they have been established through empirical methods. Therefore, assertions that have not been established through observation and experiment are considered theories or hypotheses.

As science cannot be sure about the future, it makes no definite predictions and bases all of its investigations on doubt. But Prophet Muhammad, taught by God the All-Knowing, made many decisive predictions, most of which have come true and the rest of which are waiting for their time to come true. Many Qur'anic verses point to established facts "discovered" by science only recently. The Qur'an mentions many important issues of creation and a great number of natural phenomena that no one, let alone an unlettered person, could have known about 14 centuries ago. Furthermore, as explained below, the Qur'an alludes to the farthest reach of science through the Prophets' miracles, for science originated in the Knowledge of the All-Knowing One.

The Civilization That Islam Created

The conflict of science and religion in the West dates back to the thirteenth century. The essential character of the Catholic Church's version of Christianity caused nature to be condemned as a veil separating humanity from God and cursed the knowledge of nature. As a result, science did not advance during the Middle Ages (known as the Dark Ages in European history).

However, during the same period a magnificent civilization was flourishing in the Muslim East. Obeying the Qur'anic injunctions, Muslims studied the Book of Divine Revelation (the Qur'an) and the Book of Creation (the universe) and founded the most magnificent civilization of human history. Scholars from all over the old world benefited from the centers of higher learning at Damascus, Bukhara, Baghdad, Cairo, Fez, Qairawan, Zeitona, Cordoba, Sicily, Isfahan, Delhi, and elsewhere throughout the Muslim world. Historians liken the Muslim world of that time to a beehive, for roads were full of students, scientists, and scholars traveling from one center of learning to another. Such world-renowned figures as al-Kindi, al-Khwarizmi, al-Farabi, Ibn Sina, al-Mas'udi, Ibn al-Haytham, al-Biruni, al-Ghazzali, Nasir al-Din al-Tusi, al-Zahrawi and many others shone like stars in the firmament of the sciences.

In his multi-volume *Introduction to the History of Science* (1927-48), George Sarton divided his work into 50-year periods, naming each chapter after that period's most eminent scientist. For the middle of the eighth century CE/second century AH to the twelfth century CE/fifth century AH, each of the seven 50-year periods carries the name of a Muslim scientist: "the Time of al-Khwarizmi," "the Time of al-Biruni," and so on. Within these chapters, Sarton lists 100 important Muslim scientists and their principal works.

John Davenport, a leading scientist, observed:

> It must be owned that all the knowledge whether of Physics, Astronomy, Philosophy or Mathematics, which flourished in Europe from the 10th century was originally derived from the Arabian schools, and the Spanish Saracen may be looked upon as the father of European philosophy.[1]

Bertrand Russell, the famous British philosopher, wrote:

> The supremacy of the East was not only military. Science, philosophy, poetry, and the arts, all flourished in the Muhammedan world at a time when Europe was sunk in barbarism. Europeans,

with unpardonable insularity, call this period "the Dark Ages": but it was only in Europe that it was dark—indeed only in Christian Europe, for Spain, which was Mohammedan, had a brilliant culture.[2]

Robert Briffault, the renowned historian, acknowledges in his *The Making of Humanity*:

It is highly probable that but for the Arabs, modern European civilization would have never assumed that character which has enabled it to transcend all previous phases of evolution. For although there is not a single aspect of human growth in which the decisive influence of Islamic culture is not traceable, nowhere is it so clear and momentous as in the genesis of that power which constitutes the paramount distinctive force of the modern world and the supreme course of its victory—natural sciences and the scientific spirit... What we call sciences arose in Europe as a result of a new spirit of inquiry; of new methods of investigation, of the method of experiment, observation, measurement, of the development of Mathematics in a form unknown to the Greeks. That spirit and those methods were introduced into the European world by the Arabs.[3]

L. Stoddard acknowledges that for its first 5 centuries, the realm of Islam was the most civilized and progressive portion of the world. Studded with splendid cities, gracious mosques, and quiet universities, the Muslim East offered a striking contrast to the West, which was sunk in the night of the Dark Ages.[4]

This bright civilization progressed until it suffered terrible disasters coming like huge overlapping waves: the European Crusades (1097-1270) and the Mongol invasion (1216-58). These disasters continued for centuries, until the Muslim government in Baghdad collapsed (1258) and the history of Islam entered a new phase in the thirteenth century with the Ottoman Turks. Islamic civilization was still vigorous and remained far ahead of the West in economic and military fields until the eighteenth century, despite (from the sixteenth century onward) losing ground to it in the sciences.

In the tenth century, Muslim Cordoba was Europe's most civilized city, the wonder and admiration of the world. Travelers from the north heard with something like fear of the city that contained 70 libraries with hundreds of thousands of volumes and 900 public baths. Whenever the rulers of Leon, Navarre, or Barcelona needed a surgeon, architect, dressmaker, or musician, they contacted Cordoba.[5] Muslim literary prestige was so great in Spain that the Bible and the liturgy had to be translated into Arabic for the indigenous Christian community. The account given by Alvaro, a zealous Christian writer, shows vividly how even non-Muslim Spaniards were attracted to Arab/Muslim literature:

> My fellow Christians delight in the poems and romances of the Arabs. They study the works of Muhammadan theologians and philosophers, not in order to refute them, but to acquire a correct and elegant Arabic style. Where today can a layman be found who reads the Latin commentaries on holy Scriptures? Who is there that studies the Gospels, the Prophets, the Apostles? Alas, the young Christians who are the most conspicuous for their talents have no knowledge of any literature or language save the Arabic; they read and study with avidity Arabian books; they amass whole libraries of them at a vast cost, and they everywhere sing the praises of the Arabian world.[6]

If the purpose of education and civilization is to raise people's pride, dignity, and honor so that they can improve their state and consequently the state of society, Islamic civilization has proven its value. Many writers have discussed Islam's ability to transform the societies with which it comes into contact. For example, in his speech delivered at the Church Congress of England about Islam's effects and influence upon people, Isaac Taylor said:

> When Muhammadanism is embraced, paganism, fetishism, infanticide and witchcraft disappear. Filth is replaced by cleanliness and the new convert acquires personal dignity and self-respect. Immodest dances and promiscuous intercourse of the sexes cease; female chastity is rewarded as a virtue; industry replaces idleness; licence gives place to law; order and sobriety prevail; blood feuds, cruelty to animals and slaves are eradicated. Islam swept away corruption and superstitions. Islam was a revolt against empty polemics. It gave hope to the slave, broth-

erhood to mankind, and recognition to the fundamental facts of human nature. The virtues which Islam inculcates are temperance, cleanliness, chastity, justice, fortitude, courage, benevolence, hospitality, veracity and resignation ... Islam preaches a practical brotherhood, the social equality of all Muslims. Slavery is not part of the creed of Islam. Polygamy is a more difficult question. Moses did not prohibit it. It was practised by David and it is not directly forbidden in the New Testament. Muhammad limited the unbounded licence of polygamy. It is the exception rather than the rule ... In resignation to God's Will, temperance, chastity, veracity and in brotherhood of believers they (the Muslims) set us a pattern which we should do well to follow. Islam has abolished drunkenness, gambling and prostitution, the three curses of the Christian lands. Islam has done more for civilization than Christianity. The conquest of one-third of the earth to his (Muhammad's) creed was a miracle.[7]

Science and the Modern Scientific Approach

I have given a lengthy introduction to this subject to clarify one aspect: the conflicting attitudes in the Muslim world about the relationship of Islam and science.

For many years, swayed by Western dominion over their lands, a dominion attributed to superior science and technology, some Muslim intellectuals accused Islam itself as [being] the cause of the backwardness of Muslim peoples. Having forgotten the 11 centuries or more of Islamic supremacy, they thought and wrote as if the history of Islam had only begun in the eighteenth century. Further, they made the deplorable mistake of identifying the relationship between science and religion in general in the specific terms of the relationship between science and Christianity. They did not bother to make even a superficial study of Islam and its long history.

In contrast to this, other contemporary Muslim intellectuals follow some of their Western counterparts in condemning science and technology outright and adopt an almost purely idealistic attitude. They do this after seeing the disasters—atomic bombs, mass murders, environmental pollution, loss of all moral and spiritual values, the "delirium" from which modern people suffer, and so on—that science and technology have brought to humanity, the shortcomings and mistakes of the purely scientific approach has made in seeking the truth, and the failure of science and technology to bring humanity happiness. However, Islam is the middle way. It does not reject, condemn, or "deify" the modern scientific approach.

Science has been the most revered fetish or idol of modern people for nearly 200 years. Scientists once believed that they could explain every phenomenon through science and the law of causality. However, modern physics destroyed the theoretical foundations of mechanical physics and revealed that the universe is not a clockwork of certain parts working according to strict, unchanging laws of causality and absolute determinism. Rather, despite its dazzling harmony and magnificent order, it is so complex and indeterminate that unveiling one mystery causes many more appear. Thus the more we learn about the universe, the greater our ignorance of it becomes.

Experts in atomic physics say that no one can be sure that the universe will be in the same state a moment later as it is in now. Although the universe works according to certain laws, these laws are not absolute and, more interestingly, have no real or material existence. Rather, their existence is nominal, for we deduce them by observing natural events and phenomena.

Also, it is highly questionable to what extent they have a part in [the] creation and working of things. For example, scientists say that a seed, soil, air and water bring a tree into existence, although they are causes for this result. A tree's existence requires exact calculations and ratios and the pre-established relations of the seed, soil, air and water. Science should explain how this process begins and how the seeds have become diversified. But all it does is to explain how things take place, thinking it has explained the origin of existence by attributing it to nature, self-origination, necessity, or chance.

> Nature is a print or a model composed of unseen laws, but not
> a printer and composer. It is a design, not the designer; a recip-
> ient, not the agent; an order, not the one who puts in order. It
> is a collection of laws established by Divine Will, laws [that our
> minds can grasp but] that in themselves have no power or mate-
> rial reality.[8]

Attribution of existence to self-origination, necessity, or chance
is delusion, for we can see that existence displays absolute knowledge, absolute wisdom, absolute will, and absolute power. Self-
origination, necessity, and chance are only concepts without any
material reality, and therefore cannot possess any knowledge, wisdom, will, or power.

The modern scientific approach is far from finding out and
explaining the truth behind existence. Truth is unchanging and
beyond the visible world. Its relationship with the visible, changing world is like that of the spirit and the body, of the Divine laws
of nature and natural things and events. For example, the force
of growth (a universal Divine law) is innate in all living things.
It is unchanging, and yet a tree or a person is always changing.
Likewise, regardless of how our clothing, houses, or means of
transport change over time, we remain unchanged in terms of our
essential purposes and needs as well as their impact upon our lives
and environments. All people share certain general conditions of
life and value: birth, maturity, marriage, children, and death. We all
possess some degree of will and common desires and, moreover,
share certain values: honesty, kindness, justice, courage, and so on.

Despite these facts, the modern scientific approach searches
for truth in changing nature and bases itself upon our senses'
impressions. But these impressions are deceptive and relative, for
they change from person to person. Also, not all people have the
same ability to reason. Thus it is impossible to arrive at one certain conclusion by applying deductive, inductive, or analytical reasoning to sense-based data. This is why the modern scientific
approach tries to reach facts through experimentation. However,

without pre-established axioms or premises, experiments cannot establish a fact.

Since the time of David Hume,[9] it has been generally accepted that just because an event has happened twice or a million times in two or a million different places, it must happen again. For this reason, since the collapse of classical physics Western epistemologists have spoken not of seeking the truth itself, but of seeking approximations of it. Karl Popper[10] says that we consider Newton's and Einstein's theories as science... both of them cannot be true at the same time; rather, both may be false.

Science cannot find the truth of existence's essence through empirical methods. Therefore, as Guénon puts it, science or scientists must either acknowledge that science's findings are no more than suppositions about truth and thus not recognize any certainty higher than sense perception, or blindly believe as true whatever is taught in the name of science.[11] Doubting the findings of science, modern scientists try to find a way out via agnosticism or pragmatism, thus confessing the inability of science to find truth.

Science should recognize its limits and concede that truth is unchanging and lies in the realm above the visible world. Doing so would allow it to find its real value. The relative cannot exist without the absolute. Change is possible only if the unchanging exists, and multiplicity is possible only if unity exists. Knowledge acquires permanence and stability only when it reaches the point of immutability. What is unchangeable and permanent is above the human realm. Truth is not something produced by the human mind, for it exists independently of us. Our task is to seek it.

Conflict Between Religion and Science?

Seeing religion and science or scientific studies as two conflicting disciplines is a product of the Western attitude toward religion and science. To understand this conflict, first we will discuss how science developed in the West.

While doing this, however, we should remember that the main reason for this scientific progress was the influence of Islamic civilization. Since this fact has been mentioned above, we will concentrate upon three other factors: changes in Western thinking, Protestantism, and geographical discoveries and colonialism.

CHRISTIANITY AND THE CHANGING WESTERN WAY OF THINKING: When Christianity became the Roman Empire's state religion,[12] after years of struggle and to the cost of thousands of martyrs, it found itself in a climate of prevalent Epicurean and naturalistic attitudes and sanctified human knowledge.

Jesus' teaching, subsequently known as Christianity, defeated the Roman Empire at the expense of certain doctrinal compromise. It restricted itself to love and condemned nature as a veil separating humanity from God and embarked on the path of becoming a considerably mystical religion. However, Islam and all God-revealed religions see Earth or nature as a realm in which God's Most Beautiful Names are manifested, upon which minds should reflect in order to reach God Almighty, and in which Paradise is reflected.

During the Middle Ages, dark for the west according to many, a magnificent civilization flourished in the Muslim East. As a result of Europe's contact with this civilization through the Crusades and Andalusia (Muslim Spain), Europe learned about Antiquity. Greek philosophy (especially Aristotelianism), Epicurism, and hedonism, as well as Roman naturalism, found their way into European thought. When this awakening to Antiquity via translations from Arabic and Muslim centers of learning in Andalusia and Sicily was united with Europe's envy of the Muslim East's prosperity, the ground was prepared for the Renaissance.

European ways of thinking changed greatly. An "iron wall" was built during the Crusades between European attitudes and Islam. Feeling its authority under threat due to such new ways of thinking, the Church engendered a hostile reaction to religion. The emerging intelligentsia could not find answers in the Bible to the questions posed by new developments in science and changing

world-view. Besides, they thought some of the passages to be contradictory with these developments.

For example, the Old Testament mentions 7 days like the days
of the world when describing creation: *And there was evening,
and there was morning—the first day* (Genesis 1:5). But the conception of a day as consisting of a morning and an evening is a
human concept. The Qur'an also mentions days and that God
created the universe in 6 days, but without specifying any morn-
ings or evenings. Furthermore, it presents *day* as a relative period of unknown duration:

> The angels and spirit ascend to Him in a day whereof the span
> is 50,000 years. (70:4)

> They will bid you hasten on the Doom, and God fails not His
> promise, but a day with God is 1,000 years of what you reck-
> on. (22:47)

> He directs the affair from the heaven unto Earth; then it
> ascends unto Him in a Day, whereof the measure is 1,000 years
> of what you reckon. (32:5)

There are many other factors which caused science to develop
in opposition to religion. However, such great scientists as Galileo
and Bacon[13] were not irreligious; all they wanted was a new interpretation of the Bible. Certain scientists and theologians tried to
do this. For example, Bacon favored experimental methods in
scientific investigations and defended the idea that one could
attain knowledge of heavenly things through spiritual experience. Thomas Aquinas,[14] whom some introduce as the Christian
counterpart of Imam Ghazzali, tried to reconcile Christianity
with Aristotelianism. Another theologian, Nicolas de Cusa,[15]
opposed Ptolemaic astronomy but stressed the profound meaning of the limitless universe, whose center is everywhere and whose
peripheries are nowhere. Nevertheless, the efforts of such theologians and scientists to reconcile Christianity with science could
not prevent science from finally breaking with religion. The Church's

intense opposition to scientific developments and Europe's gradual awakening to materialism were just too strong for Christianity.

As Professor Tawney says, medieval people usually sought
eternal happiness through economic activities and enterprises,
and feared economic motives that appeared in the form of strong
desires. A man had the right to gain enough money to lead a life
according to his social status, but to try to gain more meant
greed and was considered a grave sin. Wealth and property had
to be obtained legally through lawful ways and circulate among
as many people as possible.[16]

But the Renaissance changed social or even moral standards.
We also can say that such changes gave birth to the Renaissance.
A superficial glance at that period's art reveals this fundamental
change from the moral and spiritual to the material. For example, sculpture, which Sorokin[17] considers to be produced by a
desire to escape death and the mental "disease" of representing
mortals in the shape of young, immortal deities, used the female
body to model passionate desires and pleasures, deceit, sexuality and physical beauty. In Renaissance art, the Virgin Mary was
no longer an image of modesty and chastity inspiring respect and
compassion, but gradually was transformed into a woman with
physical charms. Michelangelo's David is a powerful, muscular,
and naked youth, a representation of bodily perfection.

The Renaissance man desired to be like Odysseus:[18] well-
built, comely, intelligent, powerful, and skilled in oratory. He was
convinced that this was possible through knowledge. Nevertheless,
the "God" of the Bible was jealous and forbade humanity to eat
of the fruit of knowledge:

> The Lord God took the man and put him in the Garden of
> Eden to work it and take care of it. And the Lord God com-
> manded the man: "You are free to eat from any tree in the gar-
> den; but you must not eat from the tree of the knowledge of
> good and evil, for when you eat of it you will surely die."
> (Genesis 2:15-17)

> And the Lord God said: "[By eating of the tree of the knowl-
> edge of good and evil], the man has now become like one of
> us, knowing good and evil. He must not be allowed to reach
> out his hand and take also from the tree of life and eat, and live
> for ever." So the Lord God banished him from the Garden of
> Eden to work the ground from which he had been taken.
> (Genesis 3:22-23)

These Biblical verses would be sources of antipathy to a typical Renaissance man and remind him of the Greek deities who kept the sacred fire from humanity. Thus Prometheus, who rebelled against the gods and stole their sacred fire, fired their imaginations. This change of attitude toward religion and life is a primary point in understanding the conflict between science and religion in the West.

PROTESTANTISM: According to Weber, science and technology in the West did not develop independently, for one of its driving forces was Protestantism. This Christian sect, originally a rebellion against the Catholic Church's authority, did not radically depart from Christian dogma.

Weber wrote that Protestantism is fatalistic toward history and human destiny. Everybody is born with Original Sin, and no one can be saved from eternal condemnation by his or her own deeds. Both Luther and Calvin[19] opined that God has destined only certain chosen people to be saved from eternal punishment. Such a status is indicated by that person's tireless work and continuous activity to overcome feelings of weakness and helplessness. In other words, one's wealth and success indicates how much one is loved by God. Weber asserts that the middle class' grudge against the rich and the aristocracy roused them to further earning and wealth accumulation. Earning incited consumption, consumption produced endless need, and need stimulated further work. In Weber's words, this never-ending spiral played an important role in scientific and technological progress. However, it is also behind the egotism, individualism, and self-centeredness of modern people.

GEOGRAPHIC DISCOVERIES AND COLONIALISM: Royal despotism and feudalism, when united with Church authority, suffocated people. Seemingly unable to meet their increasing needs and having easy access to oceans, Europeans began to venture overseas. Needs urge people to investigate and learn new things, and natural ways of transportation (rivers and seas) enable people in small lands to make frequent contact with surrounding and overseas lands.

The Europeans of the Renaissance embraced this chance to increase their knowledge and reach remote lands. They pursued gold, and became greedy and cruel wherever they found it. These were the people who opened the way to a ruthless colonialism. The slave trade and the almost total extermination of the indigenous peoples of America, Australia, and elsewhere became the trademark of rising capitalism and colonialism. Only after transporting the treasures of the newly invaded and conquered lands to Europe could the Industrial Revolution occur. All historians agree that James Watt invented the steamship after Bengal's (India) coal was taken to England after the Battle of Plassey (1757). The invention of the steamship (1809) marked the start of the Industrial Revolution. Today, the United States, whose population forms only 6% of the world's population, consumes 40% of the world's paper pulp, 36% of its coal, 25% of its steel, and 20% of its cotton. The developed countries together form only 16% of the world's population, yet consume 80% of its resources.

In sum, remember that a ruthless colonialism and geographic discoveries are two of the main factors behind Europe's scientific and technological advances.

The Qur'anic Approach to Science

To understand the relationship between Islam and science, consider the following analogy: Before writing a book, authors first must know what they will write. In other words, they must give it a definite form in their minds and then begin writing it. After this, they must mold the meaning or content into letters, words, sentences, paragraphs, and chapters so that others can become aware of it. However, even if this book remains only in the author's mind, it still has a kind of existence: that of meaning in the author's mind. After the book is written, people read and understand it, thereby giving it another kind of existence in their minds and memories. Even if the book is lost or withdrawn, it continues to enjoy both kinds of existence.

A palace can be built only if an architect has conceived of it and given form to this conception. Afterwards, a blueprint for the palace is made. Building means materializing the architect's conception in floors, rooms, doors, windows, and so on by using the necessary material. Even if the palace is destroyed, it remains in the architect's mind and in the memories of those who saw it.

Fethullah Gülen asserts the following:

> According to Islam, the universe resembles a book written by God, a palace built by Him to make Himself known to conscious beings—primarily us. The universe essentially exists in God's Knowledge in meaning. Creation means that through His Will, He specifies or gives a distinct character and form to that meaning as species, races, families, or individuals. Then, through His Power, He clothes each in matter so that it can exist in this time-and-space constrained material realm. After a thing ceases to exist, it continues to live in God's Knowledge and in the memories of those who saw it and through its offspring (if any). For example, a dead flower continues to exist in God's Knowledge, in the memories of those who saw it, and in its seeds.
>
> Everything has five stages or degrees of existence. First, and essentially, it exists in the Creator's Knowledge as meaning. Even if God Almighty did not create it (in the material realm), it would exist in His Knowledge as meaning, for meaning constitutes the essential existence of everything. Then, it exists in the Divine Will as a form or a plan; as a material object in the material realm; as a memory and through its offspring (if any); and, finally, its eternal existence in the other world. God Almighty will use the debris of this world to construct the other one. There, animals will continue their existence, each species through a representative of its own species, while each human being will find the eternal life designed for him or her according to how he or she lived while in this world.

The universe, which science studies, manifests God's Names and therefore has some sort of sanctity. Everything in it is a letter from God Almighty inviting us to study it and acquire knowledge of Him. Thus the universe is the collection of those letters or, as Muslim sages call it, the Divine Book of Creation issuing primarily from the Divine Attributes of Will and Power. The Qur'an, which issues from the Divine Attribute of Speech, is the universe's counterpart in written form. Just as there can be no conflict between a palace and the paper describing it, there can be no conflict between the universe and the Qur'an, for they are two expressions of the same truth. Similarly, humanity is a Divine book corresponding to the Qur'an and the universe. This is why the term used to signify a Qur'anic verse (ayat) also means events occurring within human souls and phenomena occurring in nature.[20]

What Does the Command "Read!" Signify?

The first Qur'anic revelation was:

> Read, in and with the Name of Your Lord Who created, created man of an embryo suspended. Read: And your Lord is the most Munificent, Who taught by the Pen, taught man what he knew not. (96:1-3)

This is quite significant, for the unlettered Prophet was told to read at a time when the Book did not yet exist. This means that there is another book or, rather, two books, one being the counterpart to the Book to be revealed: the universe and humanity. Believers should study the universe and humanity without prejudice. In addition, the material and psychological phenomena found in the universe and in humanity also are called signs. The imperative *Read!* is followed by *in and with the name of your Lord Who created*. This signifies three things:

- Reading (studying) the universe has its own principles, such as observation and experiment.
- *Rabb*, translated as "Lord," has many other meanings, among them educator, upbringer, sustainer, giver of a certain pattern, and giver of a particular nature to each enti-

ty. Our nature includes free will, whereas every other entity acts according to its assigned primordial nature, which
science calls "nature" and the "laws of nature." We are told
to discover these laws.

- Every human act, including scientific studies, should be
  performed in God's name and thus be an act of worship.
  This is the sole limit that the Qur'an and Islam place upon
  science. Any act so performed cannot be against God's
  commandments. For example, if scientific knowledge is
  pursued as worship, no one could harm humanity or allow
  an irresponsible minority to use it as a deadly weapon.
  If done only in His name, and by people aware of His
  constant supervision and knowing that they will be called
  to account before a Supreme Tribunal, science could
  change the world into a Garden of Eden.

Thus, as Seyyed Hossein Nasr emphasizes:

> ... revelation to man is inseparable from the cosmic revelation
> which is also a book of God. Islam, by refusing to separate man
> from nature and the study of nature from gnosis or its meta-
> physical dimension, has preserved an integral view of the uni-
> verse and sees in the arteries of the cosmic and natural order the
> flow of Divine grace.[21]

From the bosom of nature, humanity seeks to transcend
nature. If people learn how to contemplate nature as a mirror
reflecting a higher reality, nature itself can be an aid in this
process. This is why Islamic scholars and saints developed an
elaborate hierarchy of knowledge (e.g., physical, juridical, social,
theological, spiritual, and metaphysical) integrated by the principle of Divine Unity, and why so many Muslim scientists, among
them Ibn Sina (Avicenna), Nasir al-Din al-Tusi, Ak Shamsaddin,
and Ibrahim Haqqi of Erzurum, were well-versed in religious
sciences and either practicing Sufis or intellectually affiliated with
Islam's Sufi schools.

Ibn Sina was a physician and Peripatetic philosopher who expounded upon his Oriental philosophy that knowledge could be sought through illumination. Nasir al-Din al-Tusi, the leading mathematician and astronomer of his day, wrote an outstanding treatise on Islam's metaphysical dimension. Eleven centuries ago, Ibn Jarir al-Tabari, one of the most outstanding figures in Islamic jurisprudence, history, and Qur'anic interpretation, wrote how the winds fertilize clouds so that rain falls.

Such examples can be multiplied, but these suffice to show that observing and contemplating nature have always been core aspects of a Muslim's spiritual journey, and that science and other fields of Islamic studies have always been intimately connected. This connection is found in the Qur'an, which, as the Divine Scripture of Islam, corresponds to the macrocosmic revelation—the universe.

Does the Qur'an Allude to Scientific Facts and Developments?

Before proceeding to answer this question, based on the writings of Said Nursi and M. Fethullah Gülen, two leading Muslim scholars from Turkey, we should provide some important preliminary explanations:[22]

Considering science as opposed to religion and scientific study as separate from and independent of the Qur'an is just as mistaken as trying to reduce the Qur'an to a science textbook by showing that every new scientific theory or fact can be found in it. For example, some have claimed, especially in Turkey, that *dabbat al-ard* (a little moving creature) mentioned in Qur'an 27:82 is the virus that causes AIDS. However, this is a hasty conclusion for several reasons: The Qur'an is silent about this creature's nature; if we accept this assertion, we also must accept other venereal disease-causing bacteria or viruses; and, we cannot know whether new and more lethal viral diseases will appear in the future.

The context in which *dabbat al-ard* appears suggests that it will emerge toward the end of this world, when almost no one believes in God. So, we must not show haste in trying to find some type of correspondence between a Qur'anic verse and every new development in science and technology. Scientific theories are usually like clothes, for both are discarded after a while. Trying to show that every new scientific fact or theory can be found in the Qur'an displays the Muslim world's inferiority complex and makes science more important than the Qur'an. Each Qur'anic verse and expression has a universal content. Therefore, any time-specific interpretation can address only one aspect of that universal content.

Every interpreter, scientist, and saint prefers a particular aspect due to his or her spiritual discovery or intuition, personal evidence, or natural disposition. Besides, we accept both Newton's physics and Einstein's physics as science and therefore true. Although in absolute terms they may be false, both must contain some truth.

Causality is a veil spread by God Almighty over the rapid flux of existence so that we can plan our lives to some degree. This means that Newton's physics and Einstein's physics are only relatively true. In short, while pondering the Qur'anic verses we should consider the relative truths found in existence and our lives, for they are much more numerous than the unchanging absolute truths.

Qur'anic expressions have multiple meanings. For example, consider the verses: *He let forth the two seas that meet together, between them a barrier, they do not overpass* (55:19-20). These verses indicate all the pairs of "seas" or realms, spiritual and material, figurative and actual, from the realms of Lordship and servanthood to the spheres of necessity and contingency, from this world to the Hereafter (including this visible, corporeal world and all unseen worlds), the Pacific and Atlantic oceans, the Mediterranean and Red seas, salt water and sweet water in the seas and underground, and such large rivers as the Euphrates and Tigris that carry sweet water and the salty seas to which they flow. All of these, together with many others I do not need to mention, are included either literally or figuratively in these verses.

So even if a Qur'anic verse or expression appears to point exactly to an established scientific fact, we should not restrict its meaning to that fact. Rather, we should consider all other possible meanings and interpretations as well.

On the other hand, sometimes the Qur'an does point or allude to specific scientific developments and facts. Being the Divine Revelation that includes *everything of wet or dry* (6:59), it cannot exclude them. Indeed, it refers to them directly or indirectly, but not in the manner of science and materialistic or naturalistic philosophy.

The Qur'an is not a science textbook that has to expound upon cosmological or scientific matters; rather, it is the eternal interpretation of the Book of the Universe and the interpreter of all natural and other sciences. It comments upon the visible and invisible worlds and discloses the spiritual treasures of the Divine Beautiful Names in the heavens and Earth. The Qur'an is the key leading to an understanding of the hidden realities behind events taking place in nature and human life, and is the tongue of the hidden worlds in the manifest world.

The Qur'an is like the sun shining in the spiritual and intellectual sky of Islam. It is the sacred map of the next world; the expounder of the Divine Attributes, Names, and acts; and the educator of humanity that guides us to truth and virtue. It is a book of law and wisdom, worship and prayer, Divine commands and prohibitions. Fully satisfying our spiritual and intellectual needs, it leaves no theological, social, economic, political, or even scientific issue undiscussed, whether brief or in detail, directly or through allusion or symbols.

The Qur'an considers creation only for the sake of knowing its Creator; science considers creation only for its own sake. The Qur'an addresses humanity; science addresses only those who specialize in it. Since the Qur'an uses creation as evidence and proof to guide us, its evidence must be easily understandable to all of us non-specialists. Guidance requires that relatively unimportant things should be touched on briefly, while subtle points should be discussed as completely as possible through parables and comparisons. So that people are not confused, guidance should not change that which is obvious. If it did, how could we derive any benefit?

Like everything else, science has its source in one of God Almighty's Beautiful Names. The Name the All-Healing shines on medicine; geometry and engineering depend on the Names the All-Just, All-Shaping, and All-Harmonizing; and philosophy reflects the Name the All-Wise. As pointed out above, the Creator refers in the Qur'an to everything that He has allowed us to learn and use for our material and spiritual progress.

The Qur'an's primary aims are to make God Almighty known, open the way to belief and worship, and organize our individual and social life so that we may attain perfect happiness in both worlds. To achieve this aim, it refers to things, events, and scientific facts in proportion to their importance. Thus the Qur'an provides detailed explanations of the pillars of belief, the fundamentals of religion, the foundations of human life, and the essentials of worship, but only hints at other relatively less significant things. The meaning of a verse may be compared to a rosebud: It is hidden by successive layers of petals. A new meaning is perceived as each petal unfolds, and people discover one of those meanings according to their capacity and are satisfied with it.

Depths of Meaning in the Qur'an

The Qur'an, being the Book for every age and person, has great depths of meaning. It is an infinite ocean into which all people with knowledge and ability can dive deeply and, according to their capacity, find its pearls and coral. The passage of time only rejuvenates its scientific wisdom. Every generation discovers its wisdom anew, and its secrets continue to be revealed.

As pointed out by Said Nursi, the Qur'an mentions many apparently insignificant events that nevertheless conceal a universal principle and are presented as the tip of a general law. For example, *(He) taught Adam the names of all of them* (2:32) mentions that Adam was taught *the names* as a miracle to proclaim his superiority over angels in being favored with ruling Earth in His name (vicegerency). Although this appears to be a small and particular event, it constitutes the tip of the following universal principle: Due to humanity's comprehensive nature, all men and women were taught (or given the potential to obtain) a great deal of information. In addition, they were given a vast scientific knowledge of all aspects of the universe and an extensive knowledge of the Creator's Attributes and acts. Such abilities made us superior to angels, as well as to the heavens, Earth, and mountains, all of which refused the Supreme Trust—ego. As we agreed to bear this Trust, each person was made God's vicegerent.

Even the angels' prostration before Adam and Satan's refusal to do so, a small and particular event in the Unseen, is the tip of a most comprehensive, universally observed principle.[23] It suggests a most extensive truth: Through this event, the Qur'an informs us that most material beings in the universe and their spiritual representatives are subjugated to humanity and everready to satisfy the needs and desires of our various faculties. In addition, the Qur'an warns humanity about evil beings and their immaterial representatives, as well as the devilish inhabitants of Earth, who corrupt people's potential for perfection and seduce them into wrong paths. It also reminds people of what terrible enemies and great obstacles they will meet on their way to perfection. Thus this simple event is really an elevated discourse with all creation and humanity.

The Qur'an states that everything, wet or dry, is found in it. Is that really so? Yes, but not all people can see the truth of this assertion, for things are found at different levels. The Qur'an contains all things, either in the form of seeds, nuclei, summaries, principles, or signs, and they are found either explicitly, implicitly, allusively, vaguely, or suggestively. The form such knowledge takes depends upon the occasion, how it can best serve the Qur'an's purposes, and its connection with the context's requirements.

Examples

PROPORTIONATE GRAVITATIONAL ATTRACTION: In: *Then He turned to Heaven when it was smoke, and said to it and to Earth: "Come willingly or unwillingly." They said: "We come willingly"* (40:11), the Qur'an indicates that such cooperation is difficult. We know that the atmosphere's molecules and atoms try to escape into space, while Earth tries to attract and capture them. But for there to be an atmosphere, the motions leading to the molecules' escape must be counterbalanced by Earth's gravitational attraction.

This condition is almost impossible to fulfill. From the standpoint of geophysics, these conditions require that three important balances be preserved: atmospheric temperature, Earth's proportionate gravitational attraction, and the non-violation of this balance by various radiant energies arriving from space. The Qur'an expresses these facts in the verse mentioned above. That such almost impossible conditions are fulfilled only by God's Power is indicated in: *They said: "We come willingly."*

THE STAGES AN EMBRYO UNDERGOES IN THE WOMB: We read:

> We created man from a quintessence (of clay). Then We placed him as (a drop of) sperm in a place of rest, firmly fixed. Then We made the sperm into a clot of congealed blood. Then of that clot We made a lump (embryo); then We made out of that lump bones and clothed the bones with flesh. Then We developed out of it a new (distinct, individual) creature. (23:12-14)

These verses describe all of the stages that a human embryo undergoes in the womb until it becomes a human being. This information, given 14 centuries ago, now has been confirmed by embryologists and thus proves the Qur'an's Divine authorship and Muhammad's Prophethood.

CREATION IN PAIRS: The verse: *Glory be to Him, Who created in pairs all things that Earth produces, as well as their own selves, and many other things of which they know nothing* (36:36), after beginning by proclaiming that God duplicates nothing and has no likeness or equal, proceeds to say that all things were created in pairs. This type of existence indicates opposition simultaneously with similarity. The scientific definition of creation in pairs implies "similar opposites." The Qur'an gives three examples:

- Pairs produced by Earth (positron–electron, antiproton–proton, antineutron–neutron), those with different physical and chemical characteristics (metals and non-metals); biologically opposed pairs (male and female plants and animals), and physically opposed pairs.
- Pairs of their selves (man and woman; such personality traits as cruel–compassionate, generous–stingy; and traits that are similar but subject to opposed value judgments, such as hypocrisy–sincerity).
- Pairs about which we do not know.

The discovery of the positron and "parity" (creation in pairs), mentioned by the Qur'an 14 centuries ago, may be regarded as a turning point in contemporary physics.

THE PLANETS' SPHERICAL SHAPE AND ROTATIONS: These are indicated in: *He is the Lord of the heavens and Earth, and all that lies between them; He is the Lord of the easts* (37:15), for the concept of *the easts* introduces infinite dimensions and differs for each location on Earth. A point on Earth is in the east with respect to its western regions. Therefore the concept of *east* differs at every point on Earth, and these form an ensemble of *easts*. Besides, there are 180 points of sunrise, which means that the sun rises at one place for only 2 days in the year and thus there are 180 *easts*. And so this verse also indicates meridians, infinite dimensions, space's relativity, the planets' spherical shape, and Earth's rotation.

A BARRIER BETWEEN TWO SEAS: French scientist Jacques Cousteau[24] discovered that the Mediterranean Sea and the Atlantic Ocean have different chemical and biological constitutions. After conducting undersea investigations at the Straits of Gibraltar to explain this phenomenon, he concluded that "unexpected fresh water springs issue from the Southern and Northern coasts of Gibraltar. These water sprouts gush forth towards each other at angle of 45°, forming a reciprocal dam like the teeth of a comb. Due to this fact, the Mediterranean and the Atlantic Ocean cannot intermingle." When shown the verse: *He has let forth the two seas, that meet together. Between them a barrier, they do not overpass* (55:19-20), Cousteau was amazed.

This verse further draws our attention to the plankton composition of the seas, and to the flora and fish distributions that change with variations in temperature. Many other Qur'anic verses shed light upon scientific facts, and every person is invited to study them: *We made the Qur'an easy for reflection and study. Will anybody study and reflect?* (54:17).

A day will come when *We shall show them Our signs in the outer world and in their own selves until it will be manifest to them that it (the Qur'an) is the truth* (48:53). In the future humanity will concentrate more on science, and the Qur'an (the universe's counterpart in letters and the realm in which God's Names are manifested) will prove itself to be God's Revelation.

SCIENTIFIC DEVELOPMENTS CONNECTED WITH CERTAIN HISTORICAL EVENTS: Consider the following examples that allude to trains and electricity:

> Down with the makers of the trench of the fuel-fed fire! When they sat by it, and were themselves the witnesses of what they did to the believers. They ill-treated them for no other reason than that they believed in God, the Mighty, the All-Praised One. (85:4-8)

> Likewise, ... in the loaded fleet. And We have created for them the like thereof whereon they ride. (36:41-42)

Verses like these point to trains, while one of the many meanings and connotations that can be found in the following verse alludes to electricity:

> God is the Light of the heavens and Earth. The parable of His Light is as a niche wherein is a lamp, the lamp is in a glass. The

glass is, as it were, a shining star. Kindled from a blessed tree,
an olive, neither of the East nor of the West, whose oil would
almost glow forth (of itself) though no fire touched it: Light
upon light. God guides to His Light whom He wills. (24:35)

Further Dimensions of Science

Another way the Qur'an hints of technological advances and
marks their final development is by mentioning the Prophets'
miracles.

God Almighty sent Prophets to human communities as
leaders and vanguards of spiritual and moral progress. He also
endowed them with certain wonders and miracles, made them
masters and forerunners of humanity's material progress, and
commanded humanity to follow them absolutely.

The Qur'an encourages people to benefit from the Prophets'
spiritual and moral perfections by mentioning them, and urges
people to achieve through science what the Prophets showed to
humanity in their miracles. As was the case with spiritual and
moral attainments, material attainments and wonders were giv-
en to humanity as gifts by means of Prophetic miracles. For example, Noah built the first ship and Joseph made the first clock.
Thus both of these are Prophetic miracles given to humanity. This
is why so many guilds have adopted a Prophet as a patron or originator of their craft: sailors have Noah, watchmakers have Joseph,
and tailors have Enoch.

Since truth-seeking scholars and the science of eloquence
have agreed that each Qur'anic verse contains guidance and
instruction, those verses (which are the most brilliant) concerning these miracles should not be taken as historical events only,
but as containing numerous meanings for guidance. By mentioning these miracles, the Qur'an shows the ultimate goal of scientific and technological developments, specifies their final aims,
and urges humanity to pursue those aims. Just as the past is the
field for the future's seeds and a mirror to its potential, the future

is the time to reap the harvest of the past life and a mirror to the actual situation. Out of many examples, I give only a few:

TRAVELLING IN THE AIR: The verse: *And to Solomon (We subjugated) the wind: its morning stride was a month's journey and the evening stride was a month's journey* (34:12) mentions one of Solomon's miracles. It tells us that: "Solomon covered the distance of 2 months walk in two strides by flying through the air." Suggesting that travel by air is possible, it is telling humanity to learn how to do this and then to do it. Almighty God also is saying that "One of My servants did not obey his carnal desires, and so I mounted him on the air. If you give up laziness and benefit properly from certain of My laws in nature, you will be able to do this as well."

CENTRIFUGE AND ARTESIAN WELLS: The verse:

> When Moses asked for water for his people, We said: "Strike the rock with your staff." Then gushed forth therefrom 12 springs (so that) each tribe knew their drinking place. (2:60)

indicates that simple tools enable one to benefit from underground treasuries of Mercy. Water may be drawn out in places that are as hard as rock with a simple tool. In other words: "Since you can find Mercy's finest blessing—water—with a staff-like device, strive to find it." Through this verse, God Almighty suggests: "I gave a staff to one of My servants who relied on Me. With it, he draws forth water from wherever he wishes. If you rely on My laws of Mercy, you can obtain a similar device. So, come and do so."

One important result of scientific progress is the invention of devices that cause water to well up at most of the places where they are applied. The verse points to further goals and limits beyond that, just as the previous one specified further attainments far ahead of today's airplanes.

A CURE FOR EVERY ILLNESS: The verse: *I heal him who was born blind, and the leper, and I raise the dead by God's leave* (3:49) is about one of Jesus' miracles. It alludes to and encourages the highest level of healing with which the Lord endowed him, and suggests: "Even the most chronic ailments have a cure. So do not despair, O children of Adam. Rather, search for it and you will find it. It might even give a temporary tinge of life to death."

By this verse God Almighty means: "One of My servants renounced the world for My sake, and so I gave him two gifts: the remedy for spiritual ailments and the cure for physical sicknesses. Dead hearts were quickened through the light of guidance, and those people who were at death's door because of their illness were healed through his breath and cure. You may find the cure for all illnesses in My pharmacy in nature, where I attached many important purposes to each thing. If you search for it diligently, surely you will find it." This verse marks the final point of medical progress, a point far ahead of the present level, and urges humanity toward it.

Many other Qur'anic verses allude to the ultimate goals of scientific progress, as do some of the Prophetic Traditions. For example, the reliable sources of Tradition record the Prophet's prediction that one day a single pomegranate would be enough for as many as 20 people and that its rind would provide shade for them. He also foretold that the wheat produced in an area the size of a house's balcony would be enough to feed a family for a year.[25]

QUESTION: Why have Muslims not developed science and discovered such Qur'anic truths? Why does the West dominate them?

ANSWER: To the extent that time and the prevalent conditions allowed them to, Muslims discovered the Qur'an's truths and, obeying its injunctions, founded a magnificent civilization that lasted for many centuries.

A typical example: While explaining the meaning of: *We send the wind fertilizing, and cause water to descend from the sky, and give it you to drink* (15:22), Ibn Jarir al-Tabari (839-923) writes about how the winds fertilize clouds so that rain may form. The verse clearly mentions the winds fertilizing clouds because it is about the formation of rain. Scientists recently discovered that clouds also are charged with electricity and that rain forms only when positive and negative poles in clouds form a circuit.

In his *Al-Bahr al-Muhit*, Abu Hayyan al-Andalusi records from Abu Ja'far ibn al-Zubayr that, based upon

> *Alif Lam Mim.* The Romans have been defeated in the nearer land, and they, after their defeat, will be victorious within 9 years—God's is the command in the former case and in the latter—and in that day believers will rejoice in God's help to victory. He helps to victory whom He wills. He is the Mighty, the Merciful. (30:1-5)

Abu al-Hakim ibn Barrajan deduced the exact day, month, and year when the Muslims would recapture Jerusalem from the Crusaders (1187) long before they did so.

Islam ruled two-thirds of the old civilized world for at least 11 centuries. During its 1,400-year existence, it has confronted continual onslaughts from the East and the West—and yet it maintained its superiority until the eighteenth century! However, only when the Muslims' own moral and spiritual decay, laziness, and negligence of what was going on around them were added to these attacks did the magnificence and supremacy of Islamic civilization began to decline, until it finally collapsed soon after World War I. Military victories and a sense of superiority had persuaded Muslims to rest on their laurels and neglect further scientific research. They abandoned themselves to living their own lives and reciting the Qur'an without studying its deeper meanings.

Meanwhile, the West made great scientific and technological progress. These were borrowed from Islamic civilization. As science is, in reality, no more than the languages of the Divine Book of Creation and an aspect of religion, whoever does not study this book and benefit from it loses in this life. Such negligence was one of the main reasons why Europe conquered the Muslim world.

Modern materialistic civilization cannot endure for long, because it is materialistic and unable to satisfy our perennial needs. Such Western sociologists as Oswald Spengler have predicted its collapse, as it is against basic human nature and values. Either it will abandon itself to its inevitable decay or equip itself with Islam's creeds, moral and spiritual values, and socioeconomic principles. In other words, Muslims will rediscover that science and religion are, in essence, two aspects of the same reality. Once again they will know that being Muslim means, first of all, to represent Islam's beauties in practical life. The luminous world of the future will be founded upon the firm foundations of Islamic morality, spirituality, and its other principles.

TWO DIFFERENT FIELDS FOR SCIENCE AND RELIGION?

Christianity did not develop as a comprehensive religion encompassing all fields of life, but as a set of spiritual and moral values with a direct bearing on life's worldly aspects. This has had serious consequences for subsequent Western history. For example, in theory, Christianity condemned war but refused to recognize its reality in human history and therefore laid down no rules of conduct for it. Since such an attitude has never ended any war, the lack of religion-based rules for war has resulted in great casualties and massacres by various Western nations throughout the world.

Similarly, Christianity condemns the world and nature as a veil separating humanity from God, a view that has encouraged modern science to regard religious authority as irrelevant. Also, the dualism apparent in separating this world and the Hereafter, religion and science, spirituality and physicality, led Western thinkers and philosophers who tried to find a space for religion beside science to assign different fields to religion and science, reason and Revelation, this world and the Hereafter.

Cartesian Dualism

Descartes[26] is the person most associated with this Western dualism, for his ideas contributed to the almost complete separation of intellectual and scientific activities from religion and, in later centuries, to the Enlightenment, the mechanistic view of life, positivism, and materialism. Cartesianism provided a shelter for those who separated their search for religion in life from their search for science. It also gave rise to many misconceptions about the relationship among life, religion, and science. Those intellectuals or philosophers who did not want to forsake either religion or scientific reasoning appealed to Cartesian dualism to justify their position.

This manner of defending religion against scientific materialism still prevails among certain Muslim intellectuals. According to them, there is a world of qualities separate from a world of quantities. Science has the authority in the world of quantities and uses observation, measurement, and experimentation. But in the world of qualities, where observation, experimentation, and measurement do not apply, religion has the right to speak. Therefore being religious cannot contradict being scientific, for religion and science have nothing to do with each other.

Although intended to defend religion against science, Cartesian dualism makes science superior to religion. By restricting religion to a set of blindly held beliefs, it relegates it to a secondary role in practical life and thought. These beliefs cannot be subjected to research, verification, and reasoning, and thus are practically irrelevant to the world and worldly life. This attitude represents religion as being only a matter of belief or non-belief, which is totally incorrect, and "proves" that there is little difference between accepting a "true" religion and belief in any other religion or even in myths and superstitions. This dualism lies behind modern trends that consider religion, whether God-revealed or human-made, as a set of dogmas inaccessible to reason and cut off from science and the perceptible world.

But religion, especially Islam, demands rational and spiritual conviction based on thinking, reasoning, searching, and verification as opposed to blind belief. Although one can enter religion through the gate of imitation, it is never advisable to remain content with a belief based on imitation. The Qur'anic verses related to legal issues do not exceed 300, while more than 700 verses urge people to study natural phenomena and to think, reason, search, observe, take lessons, reflect, and verify. The verses concluding with: *Will you not use your reason?; Will you not think?; Will you not reflect?; Will you not take lessons?; Take lessons, O men of insight,* and the Qur'anic condemnation of non-believers as people without intellect and therefore unable to think and reflect, without eyes with which to see or ears with which to hear, are serious warnings for those who see religion as blind belief and who cannot discern the essential and unbreakable connection among religion and life, nature, reason, and science.

Modern science studies the natural world. By restricting it to the material, observable realm of existence, Cartesian dualism does not allow it to admit the possibility of other realms of existence and fields of study. This may be regarded as a way of keeping scientific inquiry factual and objective. However, this attitude frequently leads to the view that such non-material studies and their conclusions are unscientific and therefore require only belief instead of research or verification.

It also carries many into agnosticism, to either deny or at least not affirm the more profound and broader dimensions of existence beyond the material. If modern science were truly objective, it either would accept the possibility of many other truths and realms whose existence cannot be discovered by its present methods, or change its tactics and techniques and equip itself with the methods necessary to discover those realms. Science will never comprehend the full reality of existence as long as it keeps its rigidly empirical approach and methods. It is unfortunate for science that it reduces humanity and the universe to their physical existence and tries to explain all of our intellectual and spiritual activities in physical terms.

Modern science deals with nature as a structured but aimless or meaningless concurrence of material things. This is not much different from Christianity's condemnation of nature as a veil separating humanity from God. Islam, on the other hand, introduces natural phenomena, as opposed to the supra-natural ones whose existence and reality science either rejects or regards as unknowable by scientific methods, as evidence of its truth or reality. It calls people to study and reflect on them, and thereby collect the nectar of belief.

Islam views nature as the realm in which God's Beautiful Names are manifested as a set of "ladders of light" by which to reach God. Having originated from God's Attributes of Will and Power, nature is the created counterpart of the Qur'an, which originated in the Divine Attribute of Speech. So nature is a book like the Qur'an, a city or palace whose meaning is explained by a sacred pamphlet (the Qur'an). In addition, this sacred pamphlet tells humanity how to dwell in and benefit from nature.

Humanity is the third counterpart of these two books, equipped with consciousness and will. This is why such Muslim scientists as Ibn Sina (Avicenna), Zahrawi, Ibrahim Haqqi, Nasir al-Din al-Tusi, and Ak Shamsaddin were practising Sufis and well-versed in religious sciences.

Nature Displays Divine Unity

Nature, the result of the Divine Beautiful Names' manifestations and a collection of mirrors reflecting the Divine Names and Attributes, has a certain sanctity. In fact, its order and constancy are two significant proofs of Divine Unity as well as the roots of all sciences. The universe's perfect order is due to its being the work of a Single Creator, for only this fact can explain the inter-relatedness, cooperation, and solidarity among all of its parts and creatures. For example, an apple can come into existence only if the soil, air, water, and sun, as well as the apple seed's and tree's properties (e.g., germination, growth, photosynthesis, and bearing fruit) fulfill their specific roles. This means that an apple can exist only if the entire universe cooperates.

Scientists classify the order and constancy of whatever takes place in the universe as natural laws, even though the elements or properties of this order and constancy, upon which science is based, have only nominal existence. What science calls laws may well be the works or activities of God through the agency of angels.[27]

Due to its refusal to include religion in its procedures, science attributes the miraculous and purposeful creation and existence, as well as the order, harmony, and constancy prevailing therein, to two things: blind, unconscious, ignorant, and inanimate laws having only nominal existence, or else to nature, which is a passive recipient and not an active agent, an object and not a subject, and devoid of consciousness, knowledge, and will. But such order, harmony, and constancy obviously require the existence of an absolute, eternal knowledge, power, and will.

In addition, science attempts to explain existence and life through chance and necessity. The reason for such ignorance is that science regards religion as a set of dogmas requiring blind belief and therefore as unscientific or irreconcilable with itself. This unforgivable attitude and denial of creation's supra-natural dimension or its agnosticism are the result of separating science and religion.

When separated from religion, science loses its real identity and aim. According to the Qur'an, these are to study existence in the light of Divine guidance in order to understand it, to use the universe as a collection of ladders to reach the "heaven" of belief, and to improve the world and thereby help each person fulfill his or her function of Divine vicegerency on Earth by living in accordance with that belief.

As we read in 2:30-31, when God told the angels He would appoint a vicegerent on Earth, they inferred that corruption, sedition, and bloodshed would result. Why? Because vicegerency requires will, knowledge, and power. Thus they replied: *"We glorify You with Your praise and proclaim Your Holiness." The Almighty answered them: "I know what you know not."* He instructed Adam in the "names"—the names and reality of things, and thus the keys of knowledge and how to master things.

As He made us superior to angels through this knowledge, He regarded "scientific" studies to understand creation and fulfill our role of vicegerent as equal to the angels' glorification and praise. This means that scientific studies undertaken to understand creation, and thereby recognize the Creator and improve the world by establishing peace and justice, are acts of worship. Given this, Islam clearly gives a sacred meaning and religious dimension to science and scientific studies.

As the first revealed Qur'anic verse begins with *Read!* at a time when written literature and literacy in that area were rare, this command is significant. This order continues: *in the name of the Lord Who creates* (96:1), which means that we should study creation and do so in the Lord's name. The word translated as "Lord" is *Rabb*, One Who brings up, educates, trains, sustains, and raises. This signifies that creation is under God's Lordship and that we should study it thoroughly as regards its coming into existence, growing, and functioning. This is what science does.

The second important connotation is that we should study creation in God's name to please Him and in accordance with His rules. Thus scientific study should not contradict religious and moral injunctions, harm people, or change the order found in the creation and the universe. When science is used to discover the Divine laws in nature and conducted within the limits of Divine permission, it will not cause environmental pollution, massive death and destruction, or, in short, corruption on Earth. Islam does not prevent scientific studies; rather, it establishes science's moral aims and places moral restrictions upon it. It urges scientists to benefit humanity as well as other creatures and, by ordering them to work in God's name, raises what they do to acts of worship.

Separating science from religion has brought wealth and material well-being to a very small minority. But as the last two centuries have shown, there are some consequences, such as global insecurity, unhappiness, and unease due to the resulting scientific materialism, brutal oppression and colonialism, wide rifts between rich and poor people; unending global or regional wars during which millions die or are left homeless, orphaned, or widowed; merciless class rivalry; and dangerous levels of environmental pollution. Separating science and religion has resulted in numerous disasters.

Another evidence of the inseparability of science and religion, even if denied by secular science, is that Prophets were forerunners of scientific discoveries and material progress. For example, some Qur'anic interpreters infer from: *When Our command was issued and the oven boiled...* (11:40), that Noah's Ark, constructed through God's guidance, was a steamship. Sailors regard Noah as their first teacher or patron. Similarly, Joseph was the first person to make a clock and thus is considered the first teacher of clock-makers, and Enoch is given the same regard by tailors.

However, secular or materialistic science does not regard Divine Revelation as a source of knowledge or revealed knowledge as scientific. For example, it considers the Flood mentioned in all Divine Scriptures and oral (unwritten) histories of all peoples to be a myth. If this (or any other) event cannot be established through scientific methods, it will not be considered scientific, and those who say that only scientific methods can reach the truth will continue to doubt the Divine Scriptures. This amounts to denying Divine Revelation and all God-revealed religions.

Also, this will cause many historical facts and events to remain hidden, as well as the history of Middle East to be taught inaccurately, for any accurate history of the area must include the life-histories of the Prophets mentioned in the Qur'an. Despite this, secular or materialistic science causes many truths to be taught as falsehoods and many falsehoods to be presented as truths by not admitting that the Divine Revelation possesses scientific reliability. For example, the Assyrians of Iraq are presented as pagans. And yet we read in 37:147: *And We sent him to 100,000 or more,* that more than 100,000 people believed in Jonah, who, according to the Bible, lived in Nineveh, the Assyrian capital.

Separating science and religion and assigning to each a different realm of competence or relevance has caused religion to be seen as a set of myths and dogmas—blind beliefs—and science to remain in the darkness of materialism. Just as it is absolutely necessary to wed and harmonize the mind and heart or the intellect and spirit, it also is vitally important to harmonize science and religion.

LIFE IN OTHER PLACES

Science still cannot explain what life really is. This world is the arena in which God manifests His Will from behind the veil of "natural causes," but life is the result of the direct manifestation of His Name the All-Living. As long as science insists upon its positivistic—even materialistic—viewpoint, it will never penetrate the mystery of life.

Scientists restrict the concept of life to conditions on or beneath Earth's surface. Therefore, when they look for extraterrestrial life, they look for conditions that are the same or approximate to life on Earth's surface. But if they had retained a sufficient sense of the absolute wonder of life (an aspect of life's being a direct manifestation of the All-Living), they would have considered forms and conditions of life currently beyond their understanding. In their view, Said Nursi's arguments for the existence of angels and other spirit beings may not be worthy of consideration. However, the latest discoveries in deep-sea biology may persuade them to review his arguments, for at the beginning of the 1930s he wrote:

> Life perfects a thing's existence, for life is the real basis and light of existence. Consciousness, in turn, is the light of life.... Since life and consciousness are so important, and a perfect harmony prevails over all creation, the universe displays a firm cohesion. As our small rotating planet is full of countless living and intelligent beings, those heavenly castles and lofty constellations must have conscious living inhabitants unique to them-

selves. Just as fish live in water, those spirit beings may exist in the sun's heat. Fire does not consume light; rather, fire makes light brighter. We observe that Eternal Power creates countless living beings from inert, solid substances and transforms the densest matter into subtle living compounds by life. Thus It radiates the light of life everywhere in great abundance and furnishes most things with the light of consciousness.

From this, we can conclude that the All-Powerful, All-Wise One would not make such subtle forms of matter as light and ether, which are close to and fitting for the spirit, without life and consciousness. He creates countless animate and conscious beings from light and darkness, ether and air, and even from meanings (conceived) and words (uttered). As He creates numerous animal species, He also creates different spirit creatures from subtle forms of matter. Some of these are angels, various spirit beings, and jinn.[28]

Half a century later, nearly 300 animal species, almost all of them previously unknown, have been discovered living around the hydrothermal vents that form when sea-water leaking through the ocean floor at spreading ridges is heated by the underlying magma and rushes into the cold ocean. Verena Tunniclife writes:

> All life requires energy, and nearly all life on the Earth looks to the sun as the source. But solar energy is not the only kind of energy available on the Earth. Consider the energy that drives the movement and eruption of the planet's crust. When you look at an active volcano, you are witnessing the escape of heat that has been produced by radioactive decay in the Earth's interior and is finally reaching the surface. Why should there not be biological communities associated with the same nuclear energy that moves continents and makes mountains? And why could not whole communities be fuelled by chemical, rather than, solar energy?
>
> ... Most of us associate the escape of heat from the interior of the Earth with violent events and unstable physical conditions, with extreme high temperatures and the release of toxic gasses—circumstances that are hardly conducive to life. The notion that biologic communities might spring up in a geolog-

ically active environment once seemed fantastic. And until
recently, few organisms were known to survive without a direct
or indirect way to tap the sun's energy. But such communities
do exist, and they represent one of the most startling discoveries of 20th century biology. They live in the deep ocean, under
conditions that are both severe and variable.[29]

This startling discovery contains clues to other realities that
science should consider. Prophet Muhammad states that angels
are created from light. We read in the Qur'an that God created
humanity from dried soil, wet clay, and an extract of clay, and then
made humanity His *khalifa* [one who comes after (to rule according to God's commandments)] for this planet. Many interpreters
of the Qur'an have concluded from this that jinn once ruled Earth
and were succeeded by humanity.

Starting from the clues above, it should be possible to conduct formal studies to determine the worth of such conclusions
as the following:

God first created pure light (*nur*) and then light. The process
of creation followed a gradual, regular accumulation of identi-
ties and/or a saltational sequence of abrupt leaps. Fire followed
light, and then came water and soil. God spread one existence
through another, compounding and interweaving, and created
living beings appropriate for each phase of creation. When the
universe was in a state of pure fire or some other high energy, He
created appropriate life forms. When Earth became suitable for
life, He created [appropriate] plants, animals, and humanity. He
adorned every part and phase of the universe with creatures,
including living ones, appropriate for that part and phase.

Finally, just as He created innumerable beings from light,
ether, air, fire, water, and soil, so does He create Paradise or Hell
from each of our words and deeds. In other words, just as He
grows a tree from a tiny seed through particles of soil, air, and
water, so will He build the other world from the material of this
world, including Paradise and Hell, by adapting it for the other
world during the convulsions of the Day of Judgment.

THE MEANING OF EXISTENCE

Said Nursi, one of the great teachers of the essentials of Islamic belief, wrote that there are only two explanations of how a seed germinates underground and then grows into its final form: Either each atom operative in the growth process knows its exact place, functions, and environment, as well as its relations with all other atoms, cells, and larger wholes within the organism, or there is one who has such knowledge and employs each atom in the growth process that all living or non-living entities undergo.

The following simple scientific experiment helps us understand this significant argument:

> Overbeck and his co-workers at the Baylor College of Medicine in Houston were trying to practise some gene therapy techniques by seeing if they could convert albino mice into colored ones. The researcher injected a gene essential to the production of the pigment melanin into the single-cell embryo of an albino mouse. Later they bred that mouse's offspring, half of which carried the gene on one chromosome of a chromosome pair. Classic Mendelian genetics told them that roughly a quarter of the grandchildren should carry the gene on both chromosomes—should be "homozygous," in the language of genetics—and should therefore be colored.
>
> But the mice never got a chance to acquire color. "The first thing we noticed," says Overbeck, "was that we were losing about 25% of the grandchildren within a week after they were born." The explanation:
>
> The melanin-related gene that his group injected into the albino mouse embryo had inserted itself into a completely unrelated gene. An unfamiliar stretch of DNA in the middle of a gene wrecks that gene's ability to get its message read. So in the mice, it seems whatever protein the gene coded for went unproduced, whatever function the protein had went undone, and the stomach, heart, liver, and spleen all wound up in the wrong place. Somehow, too, the kidneys and pancreas were damaged, and that damage is apparently what killed the mice.
>
> Overbeck and his colleagues have already located the gene on a particular mouse chromosome and are now trying to pin

down its structure. That will tell them something about the structure of the protein the gene encodes, how the protein works, and when and where it is produced as the gene gets "expressed," or turned on. "Is the gene expressed everywhere, or just on the left side of the embryo or just on the right side?" Overbeck wonders, "And when does it get expressed?"

These questions will take Overbeck far from the gene-transfer experiment. "We think there are at least 100,000 genes," he points out, "so the chances of this happening were literally one in 100,000."[30]

It will take many thousands of tests, and therefore thousands of [dead] mice, for such an experiment to succeed. However, we can see that there is no trial and error in nature. Any tree seed placed in the soil germinates and becomes a tree, unless something prevents it from doing so. Likewise, a human embryo grows into a living, conscious being equipped with intellectual and spiritual faculties.

The human body is a miracle of symmetry and asymmetry. Scientists know how an embryo develops in the womb. What they cannot figure out is how the building-block atoms reaching the embryo distinguish between right and left, determine the organ's specific location, insert themselves in their proper location, and understand the extremely complicated relations and requirements among cells and organs. This process is so complicated that if a single particle required by the right eye's pupil ends up in the ear instead, the embryo could be damaged or even die.

All animate beings are made from the same elements coming from soil, air, and water. In addition, all of them are similar to each other with respect to their bodily members and organs. And yet they are almost completely unique with respect to bodily features and visage, character, desire, and ambition. This uniqueness is so reliable that people can be identified positively just by their fingerprints.

How can we explain this? There are only two alternatives: Either each atom possesses almost infinite knowledge, will, and power, or One Who has such knowledge, will, and power creates and administers each atom. However far back we go in an attempt to ascribe this to cause and effect and heredity, these two alternatives remain valid.

This first argument, frequently emphasized by Said Nursi, lost its appeal when he pointed out the following:

> Everything takes place according to a certain program and the principle of cause and effect. Why, then, should an atom have the knowledge of its place and functions, its relations with all other atoms with which it must combine and cooperate? However, I came to understand that I was trying to find an explanation for existence within existence, or seek the Creator among the created, which is impossible and totally irrational.

This is what we see in materialistic science, whether biology or physics, for it reflects upon existence from within it and is dazzled and entangled by the universe's apparent self-organization. Everything appears to happen according to certain principles and the law of cause and effect. Basing itself upon empiricism and laboratory testing, modern science attempts to discover the Creator in laboratories. In other words, it regards the Creator as a member of creation—finite and material—and thus places, whether consciously or unconsciously, scientists above the Creator. If scientists are not seeking self-deification, what is the rationale behind looking for the Creator among the created?

Given that science advances on the feet of theories, would it not be legitimate to approach existence and the act of coming into existence from the perspective of God's Existence?

In the past, Muslim theologians argued for the necessity of God based on the unacceptability of an unending chain of causes. As everything in the universe is finite and transient, everything must have a beginning and an end. Also, anything that begins and ends needs a cause or originator to bring it into existence, since nothing can originate itself. This is true of humanity as well, for even though we are the most conscious and powerful creatures, we have no part in our coming into existence, the time and place of our birth, who our family members will be, or our race or bodily features. In fact, we have only a small degree of control over our body's workings. In short, as every existent needs an originator and the chain of originators cannot regress forever, there must be an absolute originator who is self-originating, self-existent, and self-subsistent. This is God, without beginning and end, eternal.

Even if the universe's existence is attributed to evolution, causality, nature, matter, or coincidence and necessity, we cannot deny that everything displays an all-comprehensive knowledge and an absolute power and determination through its coming into existence, life, and death. As we saw in Overbeck's experiment mentioned above, a single misplaced or misdirected gene can ruin or prevent life. Given that the interconnectedness of everything from galaxies to atoms is a reality, every atom must know the entity into which it enters as well as its unique place and function in it.

And is there not a further demonstration of the existence and free operation of an all-comprehensive knowledge, and absolute power and will, namely, that atoms made up of the same bio-chemical constituents can produce unique entities and organisms through the subtlest adjustments in their pattern of mutual relationships? Is it satisfactory to explain this as heredity or coincidence, seeing that all such explanations again rest upon the same all-encompassing knowledge, absolute power, and will?

We must not be misled by the apparent fact that everything happens according to a certain program, plan, or process of causes. This process of causes is a veil spread over the flux of the universe, the ever-moving stream of events. The laws of nature that may be inferred from this process have only a nominal existence. Unless we attribute to nature the attributes we normally would attribute to its Creator, we must accept the following: In essence and reality, it is a printing mechanism instead of a printer, a design instead of a designer, a passive recipient instead of an agent, an order instead of an orderer, and a collection of nominal laws instead of a power. The same argument holds if we replace nature with matter or coincidence and necessity, the last two of which are preference of French biologist Jacques Monod.

One point that entangles and brings down all materialist and scientific explanations is eternity. In order to perceive eternity, science first must acknowledge the inevitable limitations of its being a product of human reason. We are part of existence or creation, and therefore finite beings. Since the Infinite cannot be of the same kind as the finite, finite beings cannot comprehend the Infinite. In addition, all of us are enveloped by time and space, two of the dimensions of existence. In other words, they are there together with—not before—creation. So, we can comprehend eternity only by transcending the limits of time and space. According to Kant's terminology, this cannot be attained by theoretical reason, but only by practical reason, spiritual experience or enlightenment, or one's inner conscience.

God is not dependent on time. Possessing absolute Will, He is not compelled to do or not to do anything. He created the universe, which is like a book, each sentence, word, and letter of which is interrelated with every other. By manifesting His Names, God makes this book "speak" so that we can listen to or read it. This book's original or essential meaning originates in His Knowledge. In other words, the universe existed in His Knowledge before coming into material existence. Through manifesting Will and Power in the Sphere of Knowledge, the meanings in the Knowledge appeared as the Book of the Universe's letters, words, and sentences.

The universe, which God fastened to the string of time, is the result of the Divine manifestation of Will and Power in the Sphere of Knowledge. For an existent being, coming into existence means moving from the Sphere of Knowledge to the Sphere of Power. Death transfers it to the Sphere of Knowledge again, but now it has acquired a new state proper for a new, eternal life in the other, eternal world. The analogy of a book (see the section entitled "The Qur'anic Approach to Science") which exists in its author's mind and then molded into letters explains this divine manifestation.

God has many other Names or Attributes, and therefore many kinds of manifestation. As the manifestations of His Will and Power in Knowledge primarily brought the universe into existence and still originate new life incessantly, His manifestation of Speech in the same Knowledge gave visible existence to the Qur'an, the last and most perfect Divine Scripture. Its present revealed form is, in one way, a counterpart of the universe in letters.

Just as a magnificent building and the booklet describing it indicate the architect who produced them, the Qur'an and the universe, being two different forms or kinds of Divine manifestation, are signs of the Creator. The Qur'an came from the Divine Attribute of Speech, while the universe originated from the Divine Attributes of Will and Power. Both have their sources in the Knowledge of God. Given this, any science that studies the universe or humanity cannot contradict Islam. If there is a contradiction, it is either in the scientist's mind, intention, or quality, or in an incorrect presentation of Islam.

Existence acquires meaning from God's Existence and thus gives true meaning to all things, events, and efforts to live and acquire knowledge. Even such a small thing as an apple costs the whole universe, for the sun, soil, and water must cooperate to produce it. All of humanity could not produce this apple, even if all of its members worked together to do so. Whether for the universe as a whole or a simple life within it, a great expenditure has been made in creation. In spite of this, many living things die at birth or after a few moments of life. Our average lifespan is about 60 years, even though we are the cream of creation to whom much of existence has been subjugated.

Given this, why is such a vast expenditure made for so short a lifespan? If there is not an eternal life in an eternal world, will life and every existent thing have been pointless and in vain? No, for God creates nothing without purpose. Every existent is infinitely meaningful; displays an infinite knowledge, will, and power; and is directed to a particular aim. Regardless of its appointed time, each thing is a sign pointing to and directly related to God.

Without that relation of itself to God, every entity would mean nothing and the universe would be a huge zero. If God is not recognized, if the meaning that His Existence and Creativity provide for existence is not understood, each zero would become a sort of black hole absorbing all of the Divine manifestations and beauties in an unbeliever's heart. Belief removes the dark veil from creation and manifests the meaning it carries. Through belief, each black hole changes, according to the degree of its refinement, into a shining sun, moon, or star manifesting the meaning, aim, and beauty it has been given by its Creator.

SHOOTING STARS AND THE CLASH IN THE HEAVENS

The Qur'an declares: *Verily, We have adorned the world's heaven with lamps, and We have made them missiles for the devils* (67:5).

Let's climb a five-step stairway to understand this verse.[31]

Five Steps

FIRST STEP: Just as Earth has its own inhabitants, reality and wisdom require that the heavens have theirs. Islam calls such beings angels. Despite its small size and relative insignificance, Earth is alternately filled with, emptied of, and replenished with living and conscious beings. Thus the heavens and their decorated palace-like constellations must have conscious and percipient beings. Just like humanity and jinn, those beings observe the world, study the Book of the Universe, and herald the Divine Lordship's sovereignty.

The universe's Master has embellished and ornamented it with innumerable decorations, beauties, and inscriptions, all of which require the existence of contemplative and appreciative eyes that will observe and be delighted. Beauty requires a lover, and food is given to the hungry. Humanity and jinn perform such a minute portion of this boundless duty, glorious viewing, and comprehensive worship that countless angels and spirit beings are necessary to perform these infinite and diverse duties and acts of worship.

The Creator, Who continuously creates subtle life and enlightened, percipient beings from dense soil and turbid water, must have created many conscious beings from light, even from darkness, who are worthier of a higher life and spirit.

SECOND STEP: Earth and the heavens are like two countries under one government that conducts their important relations and transactions. For example, Earth needs the light, heat, blessings, and forms of mercy (like rain) sent from the heavens. Also, as confirmed by all revealed religions and agreed upon by all saintly scholars who unveil creation's secret truths based on what they have witnessed, angels and spirit beings descend to Earth. Given this reality, we may deduce that Earth's inhabitants can ascend to the heavens.

People can travel to the heavens through their mind, vision, and imagination. Freed from or purified of their carnal and material being's gross heaviness, the spirits of Prophets and saints travel in such realms, and the spirits of ordinary people do so after death. Since those who are "lightened" and have acquired "subtlety" and spiritual refinement travel there, certain inhabitants of Earth and the air may go to the heavens if they are clothed in an "ideal" body, energetic envelope, or immaterial body or form, and are light and subtle like spirits.

Beings travel between Earth and the heavens, and important necessities for the former are sent from the latter. Given that pure spirits travel to the heavens, evil spirits attempt to do likewise, as they are physically light and subtle. But they are driven off, for they are by nature evil and unclean.

THIRD STEP: The heavens' silence and tranquillity, order and serene regularity, and vastness and radiance show that their inhabitants differ from those of Earth: They obey God and do not quarrel or dispute among themselves, for they are innocent, their realm is vast, their nature is pure, and their stations are fixed. So when devils or evil spirit beings attempt to ascend to the heavens, its pure inhabitants mobilize to repel them.

FOURTH STEP: The wisdom of Divine Lordship's sovereignty requires a sign or reflection of this important interaction and contest in the visible, material world for conscious beings. This is particularly so for humanity, whose most important duty is observing, witnessing, supervising, and acting as a herald to His significant activities in the Unseen realm.

He has made rain a sign to explain, in physical terms, His countless miracles in spring. He has made apparent (natural) causes point to His art's wonders so that He may attract the attentive gaze of the inhabitants of the heavens and Earth to witness that amazing exhibition. He displays the vast heavens as a castle, a city arrayed with towers on which sentries are posted, so that the inhabitants of the heavens and Earth may reflect on His Lordship's majesty.

Since wisdom requires the announcement of this elevated contest, there will be a sign for it. Accordingly, other than some stars used as "missiles" directed toward devils, no atmospheric or "heavenly" event seems appropriate for this announcement. This is just the case with stellar events. They are considered suitable for repulsing devils, for they resemble missiles and signal rockets fired from the formidable bastions of high castles, and, unlike other "heavenly" events, no other function is known for such events. Moreover, this function has been widely known since the time of Adam and witnessed by those who know the reality of things and events.

FIFTH STEP: There are many kinds of stars. Everything that shines in the sky can be called a star. The Majestic Creator, the Gracious Maker, created them as jewels, shining fruits of a vast tree, or floating fishes in an infinite ocean. He made them places of excursion, mounts, or dwelling places for angels. One sort of small star was created to drive off devils and kill them. Thus, firing these shooting stars to repulse devils may have three meanings:

- A sign that the law of contest also exists in the heavens.
- The heavens contain watchful guards and obedient inhabitants, as well as Divine forces, who do not like earthly evildoers mixing with and eavesdropping on them.
- Spying devils, representatives of the filth and wickedness on Earth, try to pollute the clean and pure realm of the heavens inhabited by pure beings, and spy on their talk in the name of evil spirits.[32] Shooting stars drive them from the heavens' doors.

What Does the Meteor Shower Signify?

Scientists have offered no acceptable reason for meteor showers, which occur almost annually. However, the Perseid meteor shower observed almost every year suggests that meteors are shot for certain important purposes, for they surprise observers by showing great diversity. The observations made in 1993, for example, show that the structure of such showers remains poorly understood.

> According to data given by the International Meteor Organization about the events of the 1993 shower (*Astronomy*, October 1993), the first results posted for the night of 11/12 August came from Japan. Up to 20:30 (all times UT), 11 August, the meteor rates were found to be normal. A zenithal hourly rate (ZHR) of 40 meteors per hour (m/h) was tentatively assigned to the shower at this time.
>
> Preliminary data from European observers indicated that the rates gradually increased to ZHR of order 100 m/h between 20:00, 11 August and 01:00, 12 August. Observers in France reported a noticeable increase in rates after 00:30, 12 August, with the rate being about twice that of "normal." The rates continued to climb between 01:00 and 03:00. A preliminary ZHR of 200-250 was ascribed to this period. The rates appeared to reach a maximum between 03:00 and 03:30. The ZHR at maximum was estimated to be of the order of 500. Observations

> from the Canary Islands indicated that the rates began to decline after 04:00.
>
> Higher than normal rates were reported from many observers in the U.S. and Japan. As Martin Beech commented in *Astronomy* (p. 11), the results clearly indicated that the shower did not behave as predicted. Speculation about a possible meteor storm proved incorrect. Another unexpected feature in 1993 was the high number of bright fireballs seen. Observers reported something like five times the normal level of Perseid fireballs on the night of 11/12 August. The Perseid shower once again showed how hard it is to predict meteor shower activity.

Morrison mentions that the reluctance to give up fixed ideas, as well as the stubborn resistance to accepting unfamiliar truths, is a typical human characteristic.[33] The early Greeks knew Earth was a sphere, but it took 2,000 years to convince people that this fact was true. New ideas encounter opposition, ridicule and abuse, but truth survives and is verified. Neither scientific studies nor developments in science can say why God's Existence should not be accepted. What we observe in and obtain from nature encourages us to know Him more closely and to see the strong bridge between science and religion, this world and the Hereafter, and reason and the spirit.

THE STYLES OF THE QUR'AN AND THE MOVEMENT OF THE SUN

The Qur'an seeks to explain and prove the four following truths: Divine Existence and Unity, the Resurrection, Prophethood, and Divine worship and justice. All of its explanations, injunctions, and accounts of previous peoples are meant to establish those four principles in our minds, hearts, and daily lives. To this end, just as nature is the realm in which God's Names are manifested and is therefore a collection of signs of Divine Existence and Unity, the Qur'an frequently refers to the realities of creation, natural events and things, and humanity as a part of nature and as the fruit and a sample of the Tree of Creation as a whole.

The Qur'an and Natural Phenomena

The Qur'an is not a science book. But since science deals with nature and humanity, and since science and technology constitute very important aspects of our life and are products of our mind, the Qur'an refers to them, either explicitly or implicitly or by allusion, for it contains *whatever is wet and dry*. Science deals with nature and things for their own sake and concentrates on how something happens; the Qur'an refers to them for the sake of God, for their most fundamental purpose is to serve as signs of Divine Existence and Unity and as manifestations of Divine Names, and therefore as the means of obtaining knowledge of God.

Furthermore, the Qur'an seeks to guide people and inculcate belief and high standards of morality. As the great majority of people do not have specialized knowledge about scientific facts or theories, it would be inappropriate for a book of guidance for all people and all times to refer to things and natural events in a scientific manner. For example, if the Qur'an referred to the sun as a heavenly body of such and such size, made up of gases composed of two trillion times one billion tons of matter, along with the remains of other elements, and in which for every million atoms of hydrogen there are about 85,000 helium atoms, most people would be simply bewildered or indifferent. As the comprehensive and conclusive Revelation, the Qur'an addresses all levels of understanding and intends to be understood and have belief and action follow understanding.

Since most people judge according to their sense impressions, the Qur'an uses the appropriate language and style. For example, while narrating the story of Dhu'l-Qarnayn,[34] the Qur'an says that he reached the setting place of the sun and found the sun setting in a fiery muddy spring (18:86). Of course the sun does not set in a spring. But this verse, besides hinting at many clues to certain facts that will be discovered at some time in the future, considers ordinary sense impressions.

This verse indicates several things, as follows:

- Dhu'l-Qarnayn reached a land in the west adjoining water around which there was no other visible land. Most Qur'anic commentators conclude that he reached the Atlantic Ocean.

- Dhu'l-Qarnayn did not reach the coasts of the land he conquered in the west, but advanced only so far as the point from which he could see the ocean like a spring.

- He reached that point on fiery summer day and, most probably because of the vapor rising from the ocean and the adjoining marshy land, it appeared from afar like a muddy spring.

- A subtle and important point: *'Ayn*, translated here as "spring," also means "eye" and "sun." As the Qur'an's elevated perspective causes it to look at the world from "on high" and because innumerable eyes watch the world from on high, to them the ocean appears to be no bigger than a spring.

- A subtle allusion to a time when those who believe in God will gain the upper hand in the world and, ascending to the heavens, observe the world from on high.

The Sun Moves (In Its Course) to a
Resting-place for It (36:38)

The statement just discussed concerning Dhu'l-Qarnayn comprises only five words [in its Arabic original]. All Qur'anic statements contain a great deal of explicit, implicit, or allusive information in order to satisfy all levels of understanding among all people, regardless of when and where they are living, until the Day of Judgment. Another example is the following four-word verse [in its Arabic original]: *The sun moves (in its course) to a resting-place for it* (36:38).

Before presenting a detailed analysis, remember that the sense impressions of previous people caused them to believe that the sun moved around a motionless Earth. Later developments in science and observation showed that Earth spins upon its axis and orbits the relatively motionless sun. Given this context, the Qur'an mentions the sun as moving and as an illustration of the universe's prevailing and magnificent order, a sign of God's Might and Knowledge. This statement's context is as follows:

> A sign for them is the night. We strip it of the day, and behold!, they are in darkness. And the sun moves (in its course) to a resting-place for it. That is the measuring and ordaining of the All-Mighty, the All-Knowing. And for the moon We have appointed mansions till it returns like an old shriveled palm-leaf. It is not for the sun to overtake the moon, nor does the night outstrip the day. They float, each in an orbit. (36:37-40)

Given the context, we see that the sun has a vital function in the universal order. The Qur'an uses *mustaqarr*, which means stability of the course and the place in which that stability is secured. From this, we can understand that the sun has a central position in the universe's order. By using the preposition *li* with *mustaqarr*, three meanings are given: for, to, and in. And so this verse's exact meaning is: The sun follows a route or course to a fixed place that has been determined for it and for the purpose of its (system's) stability.

In recent decades, solar astronomers have discovered that the sun is not motionless.[35] Rather, it quivers, shakes, and continually rings like a well-hit gong. The resulting vibrations reveal vital information about its deep interior and hidden layers, information that affects calculations of the universe's age. Also, knowing exactly how the sun spins internally is important in testing Einstein's theory of general relativity. Like so many other significant findings in astronomy, this one was totally unexpected. Some astronomers have commented that it is as if the sun were a symphony orchestra with all its instruments being played at once. At certain times, all of these vibrations combine to produce on the solar surface a net oscillation that is thousands of times stronger than any individual vibration.

Commenting on this verse several decades before this totally unexpected discovery, Said Nursi wrote:

As the word moves points to a style, the phrase in its course demonstrates a reality. The sun, like a vessel built of gold, travels and floats in the ocean of the heavens comprising ether and defined as a stretched and tightened wave. Although it quivers and shakes in its course or orbit, since people see it running, the Qur'an uses the word travel or float. However, since the origin of the force of gravity is movement, the sun moves and quivers in its orbit. Through this vibration, which is the wheel of its figurative movement, its satellites are attracted to it and preserved from falling and scattering. When a tree quivers, its fruits fall. But when the sun quivers and shakes, its fruits—its satellites— do not fall.

Again, wisdom requires that the sun should move and travel on its mobile throne (its course or orbit) accompanied by its soldiers (its satellites), for Divine Power has made everything moving and condemns nothing to absolute rest or motionlessness. Divine Mercy allows nothing to be condemned to inertia (the cousin of death). So the sun is free and can travel, provided it obeys God's laws and does not disturb others' freedom. Thus it is travelling, whether actually or figuratively.

But this is not the main point that the Qur'an is making, for what the Qur'an wants to get across are the facts of universal order, the wheel of which is the sun and its movement, and that the sun ensures the system's stability and orderliness.[36]

THE SUB-ATOMIC WORLD AND CREATION

In 1905, Albert Einstein published his paper "On a Heuristic Point of View Concerning the Production and Transformation of Light," which stated explicitly the quantum hypothesis for electromagnetic radiation. Another of his papers, "On the Movement of Small Particles Suspended in Stationary Liquids Required by the Molecular-Kinetic Theory of Heat," developed the theory that led to the establishment of matter's sub-atomic nature.

Following classical Newtonian physics and under the spell of scientific progress, nineteenth-century physicists claimed that they could explain every phenomenon in the universe. At an 1880 meeting held in memory of Leibniz at the Prussian Academy, E. Dubois Reymond was a bit humbler:

There have remained seven enigmas in the universe, three of
which we are unable to solve yet: The essential nature of matter and force, the essence and origin of movement, and the
nature of consciousness. The three of the rest that we can solve
although with great difficulties are: The origin of life, the order
in the universe and the apparent purpose for it, and the origin
of thought and language. As for the seventh, we can say nothing about it. It is the individual free will.[37]

The sub-atomic world threw scientists into confusion. This
world and the "quantum cosmology" that it introduces is not an
assemblage of concrete things; rather, it is made up of five elements: the electron's mass in the field in which an action occurs
(M); the proton's mass (m); the electrical charge carried by these
two elements; the energy quanta (h), defined as the amount of
energy remaining during the action's occurrence; and light's
unchanging speed (c). These five elements, and even the universe
itself, can be reduced even further—to action or energy waves
traveling through space in tiny packets or quanta. Since the quanta required for an action are unique to it and exist independently of the quanta required for the previous action, the universe's
exact state cannot be predicted. If the universe is in t_1 state now,
it cannot be predicted that it will be the same in t_2 state. Paul
Renteln, an assistant professor of physics at California State
University, writes:

> Modern physicists live in two different worlds. In one world
> we can predict the future position and momentum of a particle
> if we know its present position and momentum. This is the
> world of classical physics, including the physics described by
> Einstein's theory of gravity, the general theory of relativity. In
> the second world it is impossible to predict the exact position
> and momentum of a particle. This is the probabilistic, sub-
> atomic world of quantum mechanics. General relativity and
> quantum mechanics are the two great pillars that form the
> foundation of 20th-century physics, and yet their precepts
> assume two different kinds of universe.[38]

The real nature of this sub-atomic world and what happens within it, neither of which can be observed, make it impossible to construct any descriptive theory. In an attempt to propose his theory of quantum gravity to reconcile the two different worlds of classical and quantum physics, Renteln writes the following:

[T]he events take place at a scale far smaller than any realm yet explored by experimental physics. It is only when particles approach to within about 10 -35 meters that their gravitational interactions have to be described in the same quantum–mechanical terms that we adopt to understand the other forces of nature. This distance is 1024 times smaller than the diameter of an atom—which means that the characteristic scale of quantum gravity bears the same relation to the size of an atom as an atom bears to the size of the solar system. To probe such small distances would require a particle accelerator 1015 times more powerful than the proposed Superconducting Supercollider.

At the outset of this century, electrons surrounding the nucleus of an atom were thought to orbit the nucleus like planets in a miniature solar system. However, later researches modified that view. The electron is now understood to be more of an energy field cloud fluctuating around a nucleus.

The nucleus itself seemed to be composed of two smaller constituents—protons and neutrons. However, in the 1960s, physicists Murray Gell-Mann and George Zweig confirmed by experiments that protons and neutrons were made up of even more elementary particles, which Gell-Mann called "quarks." Quarks cannot be seen, not just because they are too small but also because they do not seem to be quite "all there."

Quarks are better described as swirls of dynamic energy, which means that solid matter is not, at its fundamental level, solid at all. Anything you hold in your hand and which seems solid is really a quivering, shimmering, lacy lattice of energy, pulsating millions of times every second as billions of fundamental particles gyrate and spin in an eternal dance. At its most fundamental level, everything is energy held together by forces of incredible power.

This is not all that makes us unable to predict even the nearest future of the universe. According to Werner Heisenberg's[39] theories, at just the time when we can know either where a particle is or how fast it is travelling, we cannot know both. This is because the very act of measuring the particle alters its behaviour. Measuring the particle's speed changes its position, and measuring its position changes its speed.

However, the unpredictability in the sub-atomic world does not change anything in our everyday, predictable world. Everything works according to the basic laws of classical Newtonian physics.[40]

Why is this so, and how should we view our world and the events that occur in it?

Scientists who believe in God's Existence and His creation of the universe suggest that God did not create the universe as a single act and then leave it to operate according to the laws He established. Rather, creation is a continuous act (*creatio continua*). In other words, existence continuously comes from, returns to, and perishes in God in a way that is very similar to the movement of energy or electricity and its illumination of our world through light bulbs. By manifesting all of His Names, God continuously creates, annihilates, and re-creates the universe. Such Muslim scholar–saints as Muhiy al-Din ibn al-'Arabi[41] and Mawlana Jalal al-Din al-Rumi called these pairs of acts "the continuous cycle of coming into existence and dying." Due to this cycle's incredible speed, the universe appears to be uniform and continuous. Rumi likens this to the rapid spinning of a staff that has a light on one of its ends. When spun at a high speed, that light appears to be a circle of light.

Unable to explain the extreme complexity of existence and the events taking place, some scientists assert that everything is in chaos and attribute the universe's formation to chance. According to them, other universes could have—but did not—formed, and so there is no reason why the universe assumed the form that it now has. As it is impossible for even three or more randomly moving unconscious things to come together by themselves to form the simplest entity, it is highly questionable whether a rational person can accept that the universe's wonderful order, according to which we can direct our lives, can be explained without attributing it to a supernatural intellect. Morrison writes:

> The proverbial penny may turn up heads ten times running and the chance of an eleventh is not expected but is still one in two, but the chance of a run of ten heads is very small. Suppose you have a bag containing one hundred marbles, ninety-nine black and one white. Shake the bag and let out one. The chance that the first marble out is the white one is exactly one in one hundred. Now put the marbles back and start over again. The chance of the white coming out is still one in a hundred, but the chance of the white coming out first twice in succession is one in ten thousand.
>
> Now try a third time, and the chance of the white coming out three times in succession is one hundred times ten thousand or one in a billion. Try another time or two and the figures become astronomical.
>
> The results of chance are as closely bound by law as the fact that two and two make four.
>
> All the nearly exact requirements of life could not be brought about on one planet at one time by chance. The size of the earth, the distance from the sun, the thickness of the earth's crust, the quantity of water, the amount of carbon dioxide, the volume of nitrogen, the emergence of man and his survival— all point to order out of chaos, to design and purpose, and to the fact that, according to the inexorable laws of mathematics, all these could not occur by chance simultaneously on one planet once in a billion times. It could so occur, but it did not so occur.[42]

Attributing the impossible to chance is a trick of the human mind, an indication of the stubborn resistance that causes it to confuse a theoretical possibility with an actual fact. For example, it is possible that the Pacific Ocean has now changed into milk, but actually it has not. A building cannot be built on a flowing stream. In the same way, God Almighty spread the veil of rapid movement over the sub-atomic world's unpredictability and made the universe dependent on what we call laws. This is why everything in the outer face of nature obeys the basic laws of classical

Newtonian physics. However, the two schools of the Ahl al-Sunna wa al-Jama'a[43] argue about whether the universe's continuous existence is due to the existence of established laws, which means that things have perpetual properties, or if God continuously creates the universe and orders each of its components do what He wants it to do at every moment.

Followers of the Maturidi School[44] assert that God established laws for the operation of the universe and the lives of things and beings, and gave things qualities and properties essential to each. For example, fire burns because God gave it the quality of burning. Sometimes and on certain occasions He may temporarily take away these qualities, as in the case of Abraham, who was not burned by the fire after he was thrown into it. We call such events miracles.

Followers of the Ash'ari School,[45] however, maintain that the universe has no perpetual, established existence and reality, and that things have no essential qualities in and of themselves. Thus God creates the universe anew each "moment" and continuously directs it by ordering each thing to do what it must do. For example, fire does not have the essential quality of burning; rather, fire burns because God orders it to do so. Since He has ordered this event so many times, we think that burning is fire's essential quality.

As we simultaneously accept the "relative" truth of Newtonian and quantum physics, we also can accept the truth of the views held by the Maturidi and Ash'ari schools. As a matter of belief, and as life at the most fundamental (sub-atomic) level of existence points out, God continuously creates, annihilates, re-creates, and directs the universe. On the practical level, life becomes impossible if we do not accept or assume the uniform continuity or stability of existence. How can we order our lives if we do not know that the sun will rise tomorrow morning or that we might die one second from now? Both events are theoretically possible, but we cannot order our lives around them.

IS THE BRAIN THE ORIGIN OF OUR MIND?

Artificial Intelligence (AI) is one of the most recently advanced scientific concepts. The associated field of study has been defined as "the study of mental faculties that encompasses computational techniques for performing tasks which apparently require intelligence when performed by humans."[46]

Modern scientific inquiry, while searching for new techniques to develop machines to do even more of the work now done by people, also is trying to finding analogues for human mental activities. Since many scientists assume that men and women are no more than physical–material entities (a complex of physical, biological, and chemical processes), they are trying to produce a complete copy of human functions. They assert that since no existing physical theory accounts for the human brain's non-computable processes, all human intellectual activities can be computed.

But Roger Penrose[47] argues against this assertion on the basis of Gödel's theorem,[48] which states that there will always be a true statement for every consistent formal system that has the power to do arithmetic. In other words, a formal system is a set of logical or computational rules. This system is termed *consistent* if it never produces contradictory statements. Yet, as human beings can see the truth of this statement, this indicates that our minds can go beyond the powers of any formal system. However, since Penrose's (and others like him) thought is confined by (materialistic) physics and therefore unable to account for non-computable processes, he faces a problem: The physical foundation of his theory is contingent upon future elaborations of the theory of quantum mechanics.

While explaining human consciousness, Penrose notes that the biggest mystery of all is how electrical activity in the brain gives rise to consciousness. It is hard to understand why an inner life should arise from the process of computation, regardless of its complexity. His proposed alternative theorizes that human consciousness results from quantum processes in micro-tubules—collapsing quantum wave functions (the mathematical functions describing a particle's position and momentum) in the protein structures found in a neuron's skeletons. But this is no more convincing than what he rejects.

The Source of Our Intellectual Activities

The main problem arises from accepting the physical body as the origin of all human intellectual activity. We face a similar difficul-ty when listing our expectations of AI. Aksoy has a simple but meaningful objection to our underlying AI-related assumptions:

> A man-made system can be very smart and artificially very intelligent, but no such system so far has been awarded a prize for its innovative abilities. It is the human being who made it who wins the prize. What is prized, what is of higher worth, is not the system but its maker or builder.[49]

Another objection is even simpler. For example, you may notice after running a spell-check program on your document that it missed some mistakes. Any sentence can contain correct-ly spelled words that are not used correctly. If you type "What is prized is not the system but its maker or builder" as "What is priced is not the system but its make or build," most people famil-iar with English will tell you at once that it contains mistakes. But the spell-check and grammar-check programs will judge it to be correct. Such examples can be multiplied for all tasks requiring an experience and understanding that cannot be analogued or translated for AI machines, but with which people can cope quite easily.

Another point worth mentioning relates to learning and edu-cation. Materialistic approaches attribute all human intellectual activities to a person's brain. If the theory of evolution is taken literally, more "developed" animals would be more developed in using their senses, faculties, or brains. But, as Dr. Yilmaz points out:

[C]ompared with a shark which can smell a drop of blood in the sea from a distance of about 25,000 feet, man is very much less developed. If we judge the degree of development according to the sense of smell, in place of men or monkeys, sharks will be the first. Whereas, with respect to the sense of seeing, eagles are much more developed than sharks, as well as more than men and monkeys. An eagle can spot a rabbit on the ground from a height of about 6,000 feet. Would it not be true for a honey-bee to say of us: "Those clumsy ones can draw with tools and only after calculations the hexagons that I can make so easily and exactly identical to one another. They cannot make so sweet and healing a substance as honey that I produce in great amounts."[50]

Again, taking the theory of evolution literally, must a more developed animal not inherit the abilities of less developed animals? If so, we should have the abilities of all animals, and apes should have the abilities of all animals further down the evolutionary chain. And, if we evolved from apes, should not the first man so evolved have inherited all the abilities and knowledge of all apes?

Here we find an interesting dilemma: All animals are born as if already educated and instructed with all the knowledge they need to survive, whereas people are born knowing almost nothing of the information and skills needed for their survival. All animals come to this world with the information or knowledge possessed by their predecessors, and there is a negligible (if any) difference between the amount of knowledge and abilities possessed by one animal and all others within its species. But people cannot inherit knowledge or pass it on to their progeny. Consequently, the amount and type of knowledge found in each person, as well as his or her level of intellectual and artistic capability, is extremely varied.

Behaviorism and Cognitivism in Learning

Materialistic and evolutionist psychologists view learning as a matter of behavioral patterning via reinforcement (behaviorism) or the storage and use of knowledge (cognitivism), but agree that the brain or neural systems do the actual learning. Thus the intellectual dimension of a person's existence consists of his or her brain. In short, they confuse human learning with what is doing the actual learning. They want us to view ourselves as a factory and accept the corollary logic that a factory built itself and works according to laws pre-determined by itself or the factories' "collective being."

They use such personal pronouns as "I," "you," or "we" when referring to those who learn, speak, think, reason, and decide, but forget that the brain is not self-aware and does not know what it is doing. They forget that it is people who study, speak about, comment on, and even operate on the brain. The result of such forgetfulness is that they consider it scientific to attribute our intellectual activities and faculties, and therefore our conscious existence, to the brain. If this is true, we should concentrate our efforts on the brain and adjust it to produce "suitable" individuals instead of spending our time and money on educating and raising our children.

Does attributing our intellectual activities to the brain mean that all of our needs, desires, expectations, feelings, pains of the past and anxieties of the future, and so on were pre-encoded in each person's brain? And, does the brain use the situations or the stimuli encountered in the outer world to bring them forth as responses?

Based on what we are asked to believe, the brain continually self-organizes, learns, and adapts throughout our lives. Understanding how millions of neurons self-organize through non-linear feedback interactions requires a full grasp of the mathematics of neural networks and of how this mathematics helps us understand the link between our brain and our behavior. Is it not an indication of vast ignorance to attribute all of our complex intellectual faculties and activities, all of our consciousness, culture, and religious life to a heap of blind, deaf, ignorant flesh, blood, and neurons—all of which are unconscious of themselves and their existence, and of what and why they are doing what they do? Does this make sense? Does such a view not indicate a denial of human free will?

Such psychologists as Tolman and Köhler opine that learning sometimes appears to be purposeful, that animals and people are aware of what is being acquired, and that they actively interpret environmental stimuli. However, they attribute such things to the brain by asserting the existence of more than one system in the brain involved in learning. In fact, all materialistic approaches only agree (consciously or unconsciously) on one point: Each person is an animal whose acts consist of his or her brain's automatic responses and who has no free will with which to direct and control his or her life.

Both behaviorists and cognitivists assert that learning is remarkably easy. Yet it is nevertheless extremely complex. Many super-sensory human faculties have a role in it: imagination, conceptualization, reasoning, comparing, retaining, remembering, confirming, conviction, and others. Each faculty gives its color to what is learned. For example, only imagination engenders falsehoods, while conceptualization is ambiguous as to what passes through it. Reasoning does not have an established view of what comes to it, and so can tailor itself to please the one doing the reasoning.

The materialistic approach cannot achieve that degree of conviction achieved by impartial reasoning and the study of real evidence, evidence that deserves to be called scientific knowledge. Rather, what materialist and evolutionist psychologists suggest may be only the product of imagination or partial (biased) reasoning.

CHAPTER 3

Humanity Between the Fall and the Ascension

HUMANITY BETWEEN THE FALL
AND THE ASCENSION

I bn Sina[1] (Avicenna) summarizes humanity's earthly life in
his poem on the human soul, as follows:

It descended upon thee from out of the regions above,
That exalted, ineffable, glorious, heavenly Dove.
'Twas concealed from the eyes of all those who its nature would ken,
Yet it wears not a veil, and is ever apparent to men.
Unwilling it sought thee and joined thee, and yet, though it grieve,
It is like to be still more unwilling thy body to leave.
It resisted and struggled, and would not be tamed in haste,
Yet it joined thee, and slowly grew used to this desolate waste,
Till, forgotten at length, as I ween, were haunts and its troth
In the heavenly gardens and groves, which to leave it was loath.
Until, when it entered the D of its downward Descent,
And to earth, to the C of its center, unwillingly went,
The eye (I) of infirmity smote it, and lo, it was hurled
Mid the sign-posts and ruined abodes of this desolate world
It weeps, when it thinks of home and the peace it possessed,
With tears welling forth from its eyes without pausing or rest,
And with plaintive mourning it broodeth like one bereft
O'er such trace of home as the fourfold winds have left.
Thick nets detain it, and strong is the cage whereby
It is held from seeking the lofty and spacious sky.
Until, when the hour of its homeward flight draws near,
And 'tis time for it to return to its ampler sphere,
It carols with joy, for the veil is raised, and it spies
Such things as cannot be witnessed by waking eyes.
On a lofty height doth it warble its songs of praise
(For even the lowliest being doth knowledge raise).
And so it returneth, aware of all hidden things

In the universe, while no stain to its garment clings.
Now why from its perch on high was it cast like this
To the lowest Nadir's gloomy and drear abyss?
Was it God who cast it forth for some purpose wise,
Concealed from the keenest seeker's inquiring eyes?
Then is its descent a discipline wise but stern,
That the things that it hath not heard it thus may learn.
So 'tis she whom Fate doth plunder, while her star
Setteth at length in a place from its rising far,
Like a gleam of lightning which over the meadows shone,
And, as though it ne'er had been, in a moment is gone.[2]

The Creator's being One requires that He be absolutely independent. God created humanity to manifest all of His Names and Attributes, and His being independent is seen in us as the desire for freedom. Therefore in this life, which the Prophet described as a few minutes' halt in the shade of a tree during a long journey and Ibn Sina likened to a flash of lightning on grass, our primary concern is freedom.

We have seen many communists, who regard life as only this-worldly and ascribe all human motivation to economic factors, sacrifice their lives for an illusory communist society. I always have considered it unreasonable that those who reject meta-economic values and eternal life sacrifice their lives, which must be their only aim, for the "economic relations" that are the means of living that life. So, there must be some other motives behind their sacrifice. We can manage without bread, but not without freedom. Nor can we easily give up our inborn human nobility. Since we are noble in creation, we pursue guidance. But sometimes the "stone" of misguidance falls on our head. As a result of our ego, we can become trapped in a vicious circle and find our inborn dignity and freedom, our nobler aspirations to justice and equality, exploited by certain power centers or leaders of communist [and other] movements.

HUMANITY'S ONTOLOGICAL NATURE

The universe, an integral composite entity of interrelated and interlinked parts, may be likened to a tree. This view is especially common in Eastern traditions, and such Muslim sages as Muhiy al-Din ibn al-'Arabi have written books on it entitled *The Tree of Creation*.

A tree grows from its seed or stone. Its entire future life and program is pre-recorded and compacted in the seed. The Creator has established such laws as germination and growth so that the seed may germinate in a suitable soil and climate and grow into a tree. They have the same meaning for the tree as a person's spirit has for himself or herself. After sowing the seed in the soil, the tree's life proceeds through certain stages to yield its fruit and, having begun in a seed, ultimately ends in another seed. This seed is almost identical with the original one and includes the tree's entire past life.

Consider this: For a book to come into being, its meaning first must exist in its author's mind. If this meaning is not written down, we still can say that the book exists but that its existence will become visible only when the author "materializes" it in a suitable form. Thus something's origin, its real existence, is not its material visible form but its meaning, which is invisible and without material existence or matter. And yet it subsists, constituting the essence of existence or creation.

Given this, the universe's real existence (the Tree of Creation) is found in its primordial form in God's Knowledge as meaning. Things come into existence in different worlds, one surrounding the other like concentric circles, by Divine Power acting on the primordial forms of things in His Knowledge and in accordance with Divine Destiny's measures. Like things reflected in different forms and dimensions in mirrors facing each other, all things or beings have different forms of existence in those worlds according to each one's specific conditions.

Muslim sages spoke of the High Empyrean World in which God Almighty manifests His Names almost without veil and thereby enables things to exist in almost pure forms. They mentioned other worlds as well, such as the World of Unconditioned Existence, the World of Symbols or Immaterial Forms, the Visible Material World, the Intermediate World (between this world and the next), and the Other or Eternal World. In this material world, things or beings exist in a hierarchy formed by elements at the bottom, and then proceed to move upward through plants, animals, certain unseen creatures like jinn, and finally reach the hierarchy's apex: humanity.

Any work points to the one who does it. For example, a book shows its writer. Similarly, all creatures come into existence through the Divine Names' manifestations and function as signs revealing the Almighty Creator or signposts leading to Him and making Him known.[3] This obviously requires the existence of one equipped with certain faculties (e.g., intellect, consciousness, and heart) who will recognize God and serve as a most comprehensive mirror to reflect Him. Other creatures, such as angels, have a certain knowledge of God but cannot reflect all of His Names and Attributes comprehensively, for they have no free will and cannot acquire a perfect knowledge of things and use them as steps to reach God. Therefore Divine Wisdom required a being to manifest all Divine Names and Attributes, primarily Knowledge and Will, in the Realm of Existence. This being—humanity—would be the Tree of Creation's furthest and most perfect fruit.

This existential reality is almost the same in the universe (as macro-cosmos), humanity (as normo-cosmos), and an atom (as micro-cosmos). Everything in the universe has been compacted in our nature, which leads Muslim sages to describe humanity as a specimen of creation. Our pure spiritual aspect corresponds to the angelic world; our memory and power of conception correspond to the Supreme Guarded Tablet, upon which all things and events are prerecorded and preserved both before and after they appear in the universe; our bodily composition corresponds to nature's main elements; our evil-commanding self corresponds to devils; and our power, lust, and certain negative feelings and qualities requiring discipline (e.g., vindictiveness, cunning, deception, greed, rapaciousness, etc.) correspond to certain animals, each of which is distinguished with one such quality.

Thus each person has two aspects: one angelic, pure, and spiritual, and the other one turned to elements, plants, and animals, for all people are "children of the world." We have been equipped with lust (e.g., for the opposite sex, children, money, earning, and comfort), anger (to protect ourselves and our values), and intellect. By nature we are fallible, forgetful, neglectful, fond of disputing, obstinate, selfish, jealous, and so on. Since our free will distinguishes us from other conscious beings, such as angels, these powers, faculties, and negative-seeming feelings are not restricted. However, to attain individual and social happiness in both worlds and to rise to higher ranks of humanity, we should restrict them according to certain precepts or channel them into virtues. For example, obstinacy can be channeled into steadfastness in right and truth, and jealousy into competition in doing good things.

Humanity is no more than our struggle against our nature's negative aspects, restricting or channeling them into virtue, and acquiring distinction with good qualities so that we may become good, worshipful servants of God and useful members of society. The Last Prophet of God, said: "I have been sent to perfect the standards and beauties of good morals."

HUMANITY IN THE COURSE OF FALLING

Many Western writers and thinkers assert that Christianity developed a spiritual, other-worldly doctrine based of love and opposed natural knowledge and learning.[4] Condemning our desire to learn as a veil separating humanity from any knowledge and love of God, assigning a "heavenly" value and quality to churches and monasteries, denying our free will before God's absolute Will, and propagating the doctrines of Original Sin and atonement caused people to avoid learning, separated them from nature, prevented them from acquiring authentic belief based on investigation, and made them see themselves as inherently fallen and sinful. Moreover, after Constantine made Christianity the Roman Empire's state religion (312), it gradually became almost identical with the Roman type of government under Pope St. Leo III (ruled 795-816) and Emperor Charlemagne (ruled 800-14). At that time, it came to be seen as blessing worldly power and thus constituted the foundation of a theocratic government.

The Renaissance developed in opposition to Christianity's view of the world, humanity, life, things, and art, and the subsequent Reformation sought to reform the Catholic Church. While Catholicism regarded humanity as desperate, wretched, and sinful by birth, Protestantism tried to reinterpret Christian dogma so that humanity could acquire the will power needed to reform itself. It held that people are sinful by birth and cannot be saved through their actions, for salvation is preordained by God and reflected in one's unceasing work. Thus people were confined within the vicious circle of working, earning, and consuming, or working to consume and consuming to work.

Following the Renaissance, Aldous Huxley's[5] *Brave New World* has been becoming more a reality in the West and less a satirical fantasy. In Huxley's new world, human beings are produced, classified, and conditioned in tubes according to their future social functions: Alpha, Beta, Gamma, Delta, and Epsilon types. The old world, in which traditional values and feelings coming from religion and religious life (e.g., fatherhood, motherhood, kinship, love, sacrifice, altruism, and chastity) prevailed has been replaced by this new one. By freeing its people from religion, morality, thought, art, production sufficient for a moderate life, and sharing and mutual helping, the new world reduced the individual and community to the functions of consumption, entertainment, and stability. But humanity's proper dignity is seen only in carrying the trust laid upon all people: the ego and freedom's risks and promises—a burden so heavy that our reason, free will, and power almost cannot bear it.

As Alexis Carrel puts it:

> ...in the modern world as established by engineers under the guidance of scientists, man lives in metropolises where he has set up factories, opened offices, founded schools and invented

various kinds of devices for amusement. The house where he lives and the office where he works are no longer dark and dingy. The devices of heating and lighting keep the temperature at the desired level and all kinds of measures have been taken against changes in weather. He is no longer oppressed by either freezing storms or suffocating heat. He no longer has the trouble of using his feet while going to work or returning home. Distances have diminished and, due to the gigantic advances in transportation and communication, the world has become like a big village. Wide highways, comfortable houses, air-conditioning devices, washing machines, fridges, electrical and electronic appliances of all kinds, modern baths, luxurious cars, computers and telecommunicative devices incite modern man to sing songs of victory—the victory won against the traditional values and nature![6]

Humanity has done all of this and can achieve much more. But we still have not solved the mysteries of our ego, learned the meaning of being human, or perceived that we are part of and have unbreakable ties with the natural environment. As Mefisto says in Goethe's *Faust*,[7] when he attempts to know any living being, he first drives away its spirit.

In order to meet our ever-increasing needs, natural science has advanced while humanity has not yet fully grasped that no person can make a blade of grass, a gnat's wing, or a single living cell.[8] Sometimes we feel like stones cast aimlessly on the desert of the world; see the world as devoid of intellect, the heavens as devoid of feelings, and existence as meaningless; and regard sacrifice and suicide as equal. We thought we could overcome life's threats and worries by coexisting with and cooperating with other people, but our selfishness and materialism do not allow us to do so sincerely.

We have submitted our ego, which we have deified before—and thereby rejected—God, to worldly enjoyment, freedom, endless desire, and the manipulations of a cheating minority who wants to continue its dominion through finding the truth in quantity and thereby making quantity superior to the truth and quality.

They have established their dominion over the majority through using certain possibilities (e.g., coming to the world earlier, cunning, deception, and wealth). We also have submitted our honor and dignity to consumption, luxury, and cynicism.

This is natural for those who have broken with God and their primordial nature. The Qur'an describes such people as more astray [and in need of guidance] than domestic animals. It is no coincidence that many Western writers describes humanity as animals: a responsible animal, a symbolizing animal, a rebellious animal, a social animal, a hypocritical animal, an imagining animal, and so on.

Trying to discover ourselves by rejecting servanthood to God (as Fromm explains) in order to be ourselves and attain our true freedom has not enabled us to escape our inborn disposition's realities and requirements or to become free of the need and emotions of worship. Fromm also points out that today we have numerous fetishes, more deities or idols than primitive people. Causality (nature) means to attain something, and desires, ambitions, power-seeking and lusts are our modern-day deities. Fetishism, totemism, ritualism, self-dedication to a party or state, and idolizing certain people are some aspects of our modern religion. Prophets have been replaced by politicians, athletes, entertainers, movie stars, and those who set fashions. Although we believe that we determine our way (of life and thinking), we are little more than robots programmed by the mass media and the oppressive minority that owns them. The temples of our religion are banks, cinemas, universities, night clubs, stadiums, and factories.[9]

We erect walls against other people, for now "man is a wolf to man." Our relations with others are no longer human, for we see others as tools to be used, enemies to be removed, or rivals to be defeated. The law of the market directs our interpersonal relations. Capitalists consider people to be no more than machines, means of production, objects to exploit. We sell ourselves like merchandise: laborers sell their labor, and businesspeople, doctors, and officials sell their skills. The answers to "What is your job?" and "How much money do you make?" determine our social standing and value. Our self-respect depends upon what other people think of us. Not being liked by anyone at all means being non-existent.

The traditional person who lived with his or her family, siblings, and near relatives has been replaced by the modern person who, as Fromm states, seeks refuge in trade unions, the power of monopolist capital, the shade of weapons, or other such things to overcome his or her weakness and helplessness. Multinationals continue to gnaw away at us to increase their earnings. People become lost in malls and are dwarfed by the crowds encountered in major metropolises. We are seen as less than even the simplest things, reduced to nothingness among skyscrapers. The sounds coming from TVs, radios, and cassette-players do not allow us to speak. Advertisements addressing our desires and passions seek to stimulate consumption and determine our taste and choice.

Contemporary arts, modern sociopolitical systems, philosophies (e.g., existentialism and structuralism), class consciousness, superior-race theories, new-world-order theses and fantasies, and humanity's tendency toward self-destruction cannot satisfy us, for we are like Faust, who studied modern science and ignored theology. In such an atmosphere, true religion cannot be allowed to be replaced by the Satanism and other occult practices (e.g., necromancy, transcendental meditation, sorcery, and fortune-telling) dealt with in bestsellers, false beliefs (e.g., reincarnation and self-proclaimed mysticism), and other trends and whims that fascinate so many Europeans and Americans. Such things cannot give humanity, the only member of creation that can ascend to the apex of true humanity, a true human identity, freedom, and personality. Instead, they rob us of those very things and so cause us to sink to the lowest possible level.

HUMAN PERFECTIBILITY

As mentioned above, a book exists first as meaning in its author's mind. To have this immaterial and yet existent book known by others, the author must put it into words, shape it into sentences, and then organize it into paragraphs, chapters, and so on. At the end of this process, it is given material form as sequences of letters on sequentially arranged pages bound together as a book.

As this example shows, a thing has different stages or degrees of existence. The stages through which a book passes might be called "worlds": the worlds of knowledge or meaning, of arranging and organizing, of matter or material forms. In the same way, the universe has different kinds of existence in different "worlds." In Eastern philosophy generally and in Islamic philosophy particularly, some of these many worlds are usually referred to as the High Empyrean Heaven, the World of Unconditioned Existence, the World of Spirits, the World of Immaterial Forms or Symbols, the Visible Material World, and the Eternal World.

Creation passes through these worlds and assumes a totally new form in the material world inhabited by humanity. Here, meaning or knowledge needs matter to come into material existence so that it can be seen or known. Since Earth is the place in which the Creator manifests all of His Names and exhibits His Works, it has a very important place in existence. Despite its small size, it is mentioned in the Qur'an together with the heavens. Earthly existence is commonly divided into four kingdoms: those of elements, vegetables, animals, and humanity. These kingdoms are interconnected, for the human body is made up of elements and has some features in common with vegetable and animal forms. Imam 'Ali defined the worldly aspect of our being by saying that each person is a child of the world.

Materialism restricts humanity's existence to our physical aspect and regards all metaphysical aspects of existence as derived from our physical aspect. However, each person is so complex and has such comprehensive faculties, desires, and feelings that attributing our metaphysical dimension to deaf, blind, ignorant, unconscious, and inert matter becomes impossible. Our imagination lets us traverse and even transcend the whole Realm of Material Existence within a few seconds. Our feelings and desires extend beyond this physical world. We love and hate, pity and cherish, feel enmity and vengeance, are pleased and dissatisfied, rejoice and grieve, and so on.

These and other similar feelings that encompass existence have different and lasting effects upon us. The pain of past misfortunes and our anxiety over the future never leave. Our needs, desires, and ambitions are infinite. So how can anyone say that this basic dimension of our existence—one that distinguishes us from all other creatures and gives each person a unique character, potential, countenance, and temperament—originates in matter? Clearly it comes from worlds far beyond this one.

God Almighty breathes a spirit into each person, making all of us mainly metaphysical beings in the physical world. Therefore we have two dimensions: worldly (e.g., physical structure as well as vegetable and animal aspects) and heavenly/metaphysical (e.g., intellect, memory, imagination, "heart," metaphysical needs and desires, morality, spiritual questing, and lofty ideals).

The complexity found in our essential being and character engenders certain general consequences. One of these is our special relation with our environment, relatives, other people, animals, and nature. Just as a tree's entire life-history and features end or are included in its fruit, so does each person include all principal aspects or features of existence within his or her own being. How could it be otherwise, given that humanity is the Tree of Creation's fruit. This essential feature must be considered in our relations with the natural environment, for our current neglect of nature is the basic reason for our ongoing environmental problems.

In addition, since we have free will and the potential to expand continually through learning and practice, the Creator did not restrict our drives or faculties (e.g., anger, lust, reason, and so on). Anger, lust, and reason are, respectively, the origins of our instincts of defense, such animal appetites as procreation, and our intelligence and intellect. Moreover, each person carries the main characteristics of every animal. For example, we can be as rapacious as a wolf and as cunning and deceiving as a fox. As the Qur'an states:

> Decked out for humanity is the passionate love of desires for the opposite sex and offspring, for hoarded treasures of gold and silver, for branded horses, cattle and plantations, for all kinds of worldly things. (3:14)

If we do not control our powers and discipline our animal characteristics, we will indulge in many vices. Undisciplined anger can result in murder, injustice, and violations of others' rights. Unbridled lust can force us to consume whatever we find, earn money in prohibited ways, and engage in actions that God has prohibited (e.g., theft, usurpation, adultery, abortion, and infanticide). Even our reason, if left unfettered, can lead to demagogy, lying, sophistry, and other deceitful practices. Humanity's ability to achieve such great scientific and technological progress has brought such unparalleled disasters as continual wars, weapons of mass destruction, and increasing environmental pollution. In short, we can become agents of our own destruction and turn our world into a dungeon if we do not control and discipline ourselves and our powers.

As we are social beings, we have to live with other people. A harmonious social life requires justice and mutual helping, which is possible only when we obey certain rules or standards of conduct that restrict and train our powers. Given that our essential needs and character have remained stable since our creation, such rules and standards must be universal, stable, and applicable for everyone regardless of time or place. It is highly questionable whether we can know what these rules and standards must be and what standards they require, for it is almost impossible for two people to agree completely on anything. If one person, family, class, nation, or powerful person were entrusted with establishing these rules and standards, the end result would be injustice and inequality. Therefore a universal or transcendent intellect is necessary.

Such an intellect can be derived only from God, as manifested in religion revealed by the Creator of existence, Who knows all things, internally and externally as well as from the largest to the smallest, and all their interconnections from before to after time. Since not everyone can receive Divine Revelation, God Almighty used Prophets and Messengers to convey His religion to humanity. As Muhammad is the Last Prophet, there can be no other human or institutional intermediaries between God and humanity in such matters. Only those well-versed in the religious sciences can offer authoritative guidance to solve our problems. By obeying God's established rules or standards, we can restrict our powers in a way that results in finding happiness and in justice and equity among all people.

Our powers, desires, and faculties must be channeled toward virtue. For example, our lust can be satisfied through religiously acceptable ways and through reproduction. Satisfying our lust within the religious bounds of decency and chastity, instead of through debauchery and dissipation, brings happiness. Using anger to defend our sacred values (e.g., religion, intellect, life, property, and nation) is commended, whereas using it to exploit, oppress, injure, or kill others is condemned. In addition, we must restrict it within the bounds of valor and chivalry and use it to promote sacred values. As for reason, we must turn it in the virtuous direction of understanding, wisdom, and truthfulness instead of using it to deceive others for our own selfish advantage.

Feelings that are intrinsic to our nature, such as jealousy, hatred, enmity, hypocrisy, and ostentation, must be trained and directed toward virtue so that they do not end up consuming us. For example, jealousy must be channeled into an emulation free of rancor so that we can imitate those people who are superior to us in goodness and good deeds. Hatred and enmity should be directed primarily against our carnal self and our character's bad aspects. Hypocrisy and ostentation must be defeated, or at least directed toward showing our character's better side and competing with others in virtuous deeds, instead of virtuous words or gestures.

CREATION'S HIGHEST AIM

As regards humanity's happiness or perfectibility, we must stress that each person is more than just a body and an intellect, for each man and woman also has a spirit that must be satisfied in order to find true happiness. We can find spiritual satisfaction only through belief in God Almighty and our aspiration to reach Him and thereby gain eternal happiness in the other world. The physical world, our carnal self, time, and place are the thick walls of our worldly dungeon. If we remain confined within them, we can never find happiness or lead a happy life. We can escape or be freed only through belief and regular worship and by refraining from sin. As Said Nursi writes:

> Belief in God is creation's highest aim and most sublime result, and humanity's most exalted rank is knowledge of Him. The most radiant happiness and sweetest bounty for jinn and humanity is love of God contained within knowledge of God. The human spirit's purest joy and the human heart's sheerest delight is spiritual ecstasy contained within love of God. All true happiness, pure joy, sweet bounties, and unclouded pleasures are contained within knowledge and love of God. Those who truly know and love God can receive endless happiness, bounties, enlightenment, and mysteries. Those who do not are afflicted with endless spiritual and material misery, pain, and fear. If any person were allowed to rule this world, despite his or her being powerless, miserable, and unprotected amid other purposeless people in this world, what would its true worth be?
>
> People who do not recognize their Owner and discover their Master are miserable and bewildered. But those who do, and then take refuge in His Mercy and rely on His Power, see this desolate world transformed into a place of rest and felicity, a place of exchange for the Hereafter.[10]

SERVING GOD OR EGO

In sum, our real happiness lies in serving God, an activity that does not reduce us. As Said Nursi points out, those who rebel against God and rely on themselves or science and technology may develop into Pharaoh-like tyrants, but they also abase them-selves to even the lowest level if doing so suits their purpose. Such people may be stubborn and unyielding, but so wretched that they accept endless degradation for the sake of a single pleasure; unbending but so mean that they kiss the feet of devilish people for the sake of some base advantage; so conceited and domineer-ing, but reduce themselves to impotent, vainglorious tyrants since they can find no point of support in their heart; self-centered egoists who strive to gratify their material, carnal desires and pursue their personal interests.

Sincere servants of God do not degrade themselves by bow-ing in adoration or humiliation before even the greatest mem-ber of creation. Dignified servants, they worship God for no other reason or reward than that He alone deserves it; modest, mild, and gentle, they do not lower themselves voluntarily before that which is not God; weak and needy, and aware of these facts, they remain independent of others (they rely on their Munificent Owner's wealth), and powerful (they rely on their Master's infi-nite Power). They act and strive purely for God's sake and good pleasure, and to equip themselves with virtue.

To be good and virtuous servants of God Almighty, and thereby find true happiness, we must struggle with our carnal self in order to use our will correctly. Life can find its true meaning only in this arena of sacred struggle, for only this struggle allows life to evolve and be perfected.

The pleasure of this struggle lies in itself. It is like climbing an upward path, for walking on a flat surface gives no pleasure. How-ever, people who continue to walk uphill until they reach the sum-mit and wipe the sweat from their brows experience the great pleasure of achievement. Without winter, spring would not be so beautiful. Thus our true happiness and the real pleasure of life lie in struggling against temptation and defeating our evil-command-ing selves and Satan. This is how we rise along the path of perfect-ibility toward the heavens, endless and eternal happiness and pleasure, being truly human and recovering our primordial or original state as creation's best pattern and Paradise's eternal inhabitants.

KANT, SCHELER, AND SAID NURSI ON HUMANITY

In this article, I will analyze the views of three major philosophers on the relationship between God and humanity.

Kant, God, and Humanity

Kant was perhaps the foremost figure in the rationalism and enlightenment movements of eighteenth-century Europe. Descartes, the French mathematician and philosopher, was the leading exponent of the science–religion dualism that characterized the Renaissance. Kant performed a similar role as the "father" of the humanity–mind dualism in existence. We can see this same dualism, albeit indirectly, in his perspective on humanity and Scheler's[11] philosophical anthropology.

According to Kant, each person has a natural side and a mental side. Our feelings, inclinations, desires, consciousness, and emotions make up our natural side. At this point, we unite with the natural realm and animals and, like them, are under the influence of natural laws. But our mental side, which makes us human and creatures with free will, makes us superior to all other parts of creation.

Each person represents the union of natural and mental existence and, in contrast to animals, does not come to this world with the knowledge and abilities that they will need to survive here. Animals are born with whatever they need to survive, as if another intelligence had equipped them with things like horns, claws, teeth, and all necessary knowledge and instincts.

But people are born as "creatures gathering all deprivations within their egos." We have been endowed with intelligence, a will that is connected to intelligence, and a nature that does nothing unnecessary and does not waste any material used for the attainment of goals. We must accomplish, on our own, all that is above our animal-like existence without following our instincts.

We are expected to pursue only that happiness that we can obtain through our intelligence. Since we are equipped with and depend upon intelligence, we cannot be ruled by our instincts or equipped with natural knowledge alone. We must provide everything for ourselves, from food to clothing and from transportation to safety.

Kant writes that we enter this world with undeveloped skills and talents and thus require immediate training and education. A long childhood means that others must train and take care of us. We have to discover all human capabilities slowly and through our own efforts. This is why one generation educates another, for education changes an animal into a person and thereby enables them to transcend their animal inclinations, become truly human, and fulfill the purpose of human existence. By indicating the boundaries of their action and activities, education protects them from danger and from running around empty-headed. By disciplining their animal side, education also prevents them from becoming wild.

Destiny gave animals whatever they need to survive from the beginning, but gave them no knowledge of good and evil. Only we possess such knowledge, for Destiny wanted us to bring forth good on our own, as if It told us: "Go into the world. I have given you whatever you need to do good. Discover those skills, for your happiness and unhappiness are in your hands."

Education also has a role to play here. All good in the world is a product of good education. Given this, we should discover our centers of good and allow them to function freely, instead of transforming them into sources of evil. Our intelligence makes us human, and our discovery of this depends upon education.

Kant, who divided humanity into a *natural creature* and an *independent intelligent creature*, also divided existence into the *visible world* and the *independent Realm of Intelligence*, both of which form the visible world's foundation. While we comprehend the visible world with what Kant calls the *intellect* (a faculty using the senses), we comprehend the *independent realm* with *intelligence*. There are two types of intelligence: pure and practical. In the field of natural existence, pure intelligence obeys determinist laws, makes deductions about special situations according to general principles, and receives *a priori* information. The independent world, which does not obey determinist laws, is examined by practical intelligence.

The success of pure intelligence in the experiential world is greater than that of animals. But here, the only difference between humanity and animals is our practical intelligence, for that is what makes us what we are. Each person contains a center of practical intelligence and is responsible for discovering it. The findings of practical intelligence are not knowledge as we know it, which is formal and can lead to fanaticism, but rather can be called the *culture of the heart*. We can say that this intelligence determines our conscience or action and direction.

Kant believed that our practical intelligence transforms us into human beings, for it admonishes us and gives us purposes that humanize our animal side while we strive to realize them. These purposes are mostly universal and unchangeable moral principles. Morality is very important for Kant. Intelligence does not need to receive these principles from the outside, for they are in the mind *a priori*. Practical intelligence is simultaneously our will and that which appoints our duties, which are directed toward realizing the purposes mentioned above.

He also views God's Existence as wholly mental, saying that we can connect ourselves with the Divine Existence through our minds. We are humanized and attain freedom based on the degree to which we can rise above our natural side, which is comprised of desire, ambition, and feelings (e.g., love and hatred).

Our activities are tied to conditions. For this reason, laws in this field are called *conditional imperatives*. For example, doctors lay down suitable conditions when giving patients medicine. But there can be no conditions for people as *numens* or individuals in this field of existence, and thus operative laws in this field are called *categorical imperatives*. Although theoretical knowledge or experimentation, observation, and experience regarding knowledge of the natural plane of existence are necessary, the intelligence (our conscience) is in control in the absolute and unchanging *numen* field. There is no experience on this plane.

According to Kant, people become human by escaping from the necessities of the phenomenal plane and practical intelligence, which determines its own actions, and thus their autonomy and freedom.

Scheler, God, and Humanity

Scheler, the founder of philosophical anthropology, was strongly influenced by Kant. But while he repeated many of Kant's ideas, he based his philosophy upon opposing Kant. He describes the discipline he founded as follows:

> The duty of philosophical anthropology is to show in the basic make-up of man's existence the source of man's success and works like language, conscience, tools, guns, justice, injustice, government, administration, art forms, myths, religion, knowledge, history, and society.

Scheler sees humanity as a creature who gathers the universe's essence within himself or herself and, along with Kant, as a dual creature comprised of physical life (an animated aspect) and *Geist* (spirit). Kant included all feelings, including love, in the natural aspect and attached little value to them. However, Scheler accepts love as a very important component of *Geist*, the faculty equivalent to Kant's *intelligence*.

Our physical nature consists of emotion (causing action, compulsory power), instinct, memory tied to associations, and intelligence and choice. Our feelings are a union of compulsion and inclinations. We share some compulsions with plants, such as getting sufficient nutrition, breathing, and reproducing. Instincts forming the second level of our physical life should be meaningful for us, be in harmony, perpetuate the species, carry a character that can develop naturally over time, and transcend the sum of our experiences. Such instincts, which we have in common with animals, express perfection.

Memory is the third level of human physical life. When based on the constant repetition of imitated things, it is called tradition. This is the type of memory possessed by animals. In addition to this, our type of memory is associative and thus allows us to recall things. The basis of this ability is comprised of conditioned reflexes that allow the development of customs unique to humanity. Intelligence is the ability to grasp and penetrate every new situation suddenly, and is accompanied by the ability to choose.

Scheler's *Geist* is, first of all, an independent attribute of Divine Existence that reveals the difference between true humans and animals by separating a thing's essence from its existence. Thus the "matter" of *Geist* is the subject of real human qualities. In addition, *Geist* also contains the faculties of idealization (the ability to present and comprehend the essence as an idea) and reduction (the ability to penetrate the essential in the shell of existence and distinguish real existence from appearance).

From one perspective, *Geist* is comprised of intentions and has no inherent strength or power. Scheler writes that the most important characteristic of *Geist* (God) is that It has no force or power, for *Geist* only receives power from Its relationship with the plane of physical life. In other words, It depends upon this plane to realize Itself. In Its relationship with this plane, *Geist* manifests Itself by determining our direction, showing Itself in our inclinations, and by harnessing our tendencies to restrain us.

Being tied to our inclinations, we are not free and so live like animals ruled by our inclinations to pursue sex, food, and power. But when we transcend these and assume a character personifying *Geist*'s intentions, or become a locus for realizing them, we gain true humanity. This process has certain conditions, such as understanding all manifestations of life without difficulty, finding the norm in them, and distinguishing our own and others' special features (e.g., wishes, feelings, and thoughts). Also, such a personality must consciously possess and control the body.

Scheler writes that everyone has his or her own world, meaning that each world corresponds to an individual. All of these
worlds, when taken together, correspond to God. Just as our real
existence comprises *Geist*, the foundation of existence contains a
Geist that comprehends, loves, and thinks of everything. Taken
as a whole, humanity is such a being that in our being's essential existence God begins to know, comprehend, understand,
and find salvation. Thus we participate in the existence and essence
of Divine Existence, and realize the basic traits of our own *Geist*
together with God's *Geist* and our own ideal.

He agrees with Kant that existence means duality. One side
of this duality is "the side showing qualities," the subject-matter
of science, the side endowed with definite and known specific
attributes. The other side is composed of metaphysical essence,
which one must be able to perceive in order to know. This is possible only by developing the personality. God is solely an "essence"
and thus a pure object of metaphysics. Religion is a matter of our
basic make-up and does not necessarily need to include laws.
Monotheistic religions put such matters as fear, slavery, servanthood, and father–son relationships between humanity and God.
But there really is no need for such relationships, for people feel
God in their hearts and become humanized and deified at the
same moment with God. We are creatures that continually deify
ourselves and serve God's genesis and development.[12]

General Evaluation

There are some nuances and conceptual differences between
these two philosophies. In addition, while Kant's morality is based
on restraining our physical–emotional side, Scheler's is based on
love and sensing God in the heart. His conception of religion
also has pantheistic and monistic overtones. In spite of this, their
views on humanity have no deep-rooted conflict. Since both strove
to give a place to God and religion based on Christian concepts,
as opposed to the Renaissance's positivism, they located human-

ity and existence in two separate spheres in a way resembling Descartes' dualism.

As demanded by the Enlightenment's philosophy and secular morality, they thought that the values to which we must conform should be found in our own being and conscience. Influenced by the Christian belief in the Trinity and the Father–Son unity, and based upon the ideas of reincarnation and spiritual unity with God, they transformed God into a deity having a passive relationship with existence and put humanity at the center of everything. Kant looked for our humanity and happiness in our intelligence's evolution toward the universal and unchangeable moral laws found in the conscience, not in the visible–biological–phenomenal side of our nature, desires, wishes, or other emotions.

In place of Kant's moral *a priorism*, Scheler sees happiness in *a priorism* based on love and, realizing intentions through love, participation in Divine Existence. But he does not explain how this love can be attained, how we can rise above the desire and passion of love and the "physical–vital" side of our nature, and whether we can overcome them or not.

After summarizing Said Nursi's view, the profound differences between these views will become obvious. On the one hand, in the name of philosophy, there is "conscious walking along dead-end streets, where finding the way in the labyrinth becomes increasingly difficult" and ends in philosophical obscurity, intricacy, and subjectivity. On the other hand, there is an objective, realistic, and practicable view and criteria.

Said Nursi, God, and Humanity

Said Nursi's view of humanity is derived from Islam. Given this, God is the essential basis of existence as well as its creator and maintainer through His own Eternal Existence. He exists without needing any other being's or thing's existence, and is not limited by time (in which He does not exist) or space (which He does not occupy). The universe gained existence through manifesting God's Names and Attributes. As One who does whatever He wills, God keeps the universe under His Power by manifesting His Names and Attributes. Thus everything owes its existence, life, vitality, continued existence, sustenance, growth, and all of its qualities to God. There are no exceptions. Moreover, all of these things are from God.

While God was a "Hidden Treasure," due to His pure and sacred love for His "Essence," a love worthy of and suitable for His being God, He created the universe in order to contemplate Himself. In addition to showing that the bond between the universe and God is love, the universe shows God in two ways. First, everything exists as a manifestation of His Names. To give just a few examples: We see Him as the All-Living and the Giver of Life in all animate things; as the Self-Existing and the Everlasting in the universe's continued existence; as the Just in the universe's orderliness, regularity, and amazing degree of majestic balance; as the Pure in nature's absolute cleanliness, despite the death of hundreds of thousands of animals each day; and as the Wise in the functions determined for each creature.

Everything begins and ends [in death]. Said Nursi gives the analogy of standing on a river's bank and watching its bubbles, each of which contains the sun's image, pass before us. If the river passes through a tunnel, the "tiny suns" disappear. But from our position, the sun still can be seen in the bubbles. This shows that the tiny suns in the bubbles do not belong to the bubbles themselves; rather, they are the reflections of the sun and therefore point to it. Their disappearance in the tunnel, while new ones passing by us reflect the same sun, demonstrates the sun's permanence. In the same way, the very life of all living creatures shows God's Existence and Life, and shows His Permanence by their death.

Also, everything has only limited power and is poor in its essence. Nothing is in control of itself. If we consider an apple, we see that its sustenance depends upon cooperation among the sun, air, soil, and water. Apples will be produced only if an apple tree works with other elements of the universe in a "conscious and knowledge-based" way. As these created things are devoid of any consciousness and knowledge, their needs, deficiencies, helplessness, and poverty signify God's Attributes, such as His eternal and infinite Power, Knowledge, Hearing, and Seeing. In short, the main purpose of existence is to serve as a shining mirror in which God can manifest His Names and Attributes.

God created the universe before He created humanity: from His Throne to the lower heavens, from the skies to Earth, from angels to jinn, and from inanimate creatures to plants and animals. All of these manifest His other Names and Attributes, but do not have humanity's capacity for language and speech, the same level of knowledge, or, most importantly, the level of will. Thus we were created as the Tree of Creation's fruit, the limit of existence, and the final purpose.

In Said Nursi's words, God drew an imaginary line in front of His Names and Attributes and created humanity so that all of them might be reflected upon us. Thus we took our place as the most perfect, shining, and encompassing mirror reflecting God. Being able to reflect all of His Names and Attributes means that we have feelings of magnificence and greatness as well as the desire for absolute sovereignty. From such feelings come the human ego, from which all other beings shrank (33:72).

However, since magnificence, greatness, and absolute sovereignty demand absolute power and absolute wealth, which we do not have because our power extends for only an arm's length and we are more helpless than many animals, our knowledge is limited, we can never possess absolute wealth, and our needs are infinite. While we exist as an embryo or an infant, we do nothing to attain our sustenance. When we become aware of or imagine our strength, we begin to struggle for our sustenance. This shows that our duty is to admit our helplessness, poverty, and deficiency and, after that, turn to the Possessor of absolute wealth, power, and sovereignty. We should take power and wealth only from God's Power and Wealth, bind ourselves to and worship only God, and avoid serving all things, powers, or interests that are not Him.

According to Said Nursi, humanity is the fruit of the Tree of Creation and thus contains the essence and a summary of all that exists. Each person is a sample or a model of the universe. Just as we carry the physical dimension of existence with our physical aspect, we also carry all plant and animal characteristics. Having been sent as God's vicegerent to rule Earth according to His Will, we are to cultivate it and unite in peace with the rest of the universe.

Almost every animal learns what it needs to know in another realm or is given what it needs at birth, and so jumps into the arena of life almost as soon as it is born. But we are born without knowledge and must learn everything—the laws of life, how to separate good from evil, and how to determine what is in our best interests and what is not. Moreover, we are more than physical beings composed of various emotions and longings, particularly our longing for eternity, and many intellectual and spiritual faculties. We have spiritual pains and needs that are far more numerous, deeper, intricate, and in greater need of satisfaction than our physical ones. Thus our duty is to learn and evolve through training and belief.

In addition, we have the potential to acquire many abilities by working our way through the press of time and events. Just as God, allows a hawk to attack a sparrow so that the latter will develop its strength in order to defend itself and develop new abilities, He uses events and tests so that we will develop our own potential capabilities. If we use them correctly, every desire, obsession, and feeling becomes a source of goodness.

The sources of all abilities and faculties sown in our nature can be categorized into three groups: powers of appetite, anger, and reasoning (mind). Appetite satisfies our need for eating, drinking, reproduction, and all other physical–biological desires and needs. Anger is the source and a means of self-defense, and reason is the spring or center for every mental activity.

Having given us free will, God left these forces unrestrained and free in our nature so that they could be used to test us. Thus they can lead to great personal or social oppression and unhappiness. For example, appetite can lead to illegality and immorality; anger can cause murder and oppression; and reasoning can lead to demagogy, misleading persuasion, and dialectics. And so these forces must be kept in balance. In other words, appetite must revolve around chastity, anger around courage, and reasoning around wisdom so that justice will be maintained in social life. These conditions are necessary for human happiness. But because no person, whether individually or collectively, can conceive of such a balance and of the special characteristics and factors of such a broad justice, a universal intelligence is needed—Divine Religion, which God has given to us as a gift.

Just as we are affected by sorrows of the past, so are we influenced by doubts concerning the future. As showed above, our power and knowledge is limited but our needs are endless. Life here is short, but another eternal world awaits us. As the mind, with its consciousness of the past and future, can make us the most miserable and anxious of animals when it comes to meeting our needs, we must place it under the guidance of the universal intelligence.

We must use God's Power as the intercessor for our helplessness, His infinite Knowledge for our ignorance, and His boundless Wealth for our poverty. We must find power in His Power, knowledge in His Knowledge, and wealth in His Wealth. When we can do this, all of our inherent abilities, faculties, forces, desires, and needs—even such feelings that at first appear absolutely bad (e.g., jealousy and passion)—can open a door to virtue and become stepping stones. For example, jealousy can be directed toward a malice-free emulation of (or competition for) what is good, while ambition can pursue what is good and beautiful. Otherwise, we can become our own and others' worst enemy. We must not forget that the Pharaohs, Nimrods, and other infamous self-proclaimed gods and imposters were human beings.

Remarks on Human Happiness and Misery[13]

[Human beings were created of the best stature, on the best pattern of creation, and given a comprehensive potential. They have been sent to an arena of trial, where they either will rise to

[the highest rank or descend to the lowest level. These are the ways open to humanity. We are here as a miracle of power and creation's ultimate pinnacle. I shall expound the mystery of humanity's ascent and descent in five remarks.]

FIRST REMARK: We have some relationship with and are in need of most species. Our needs range into all parts of the universe, and our desires range as far as eternity. We desire a single flower as well as a whole spring, a garden as well as an eternal Paradise. We long to see our friend as well as the Majestic, All-Beautiful One. We knock on our beloved friend's door for a visit, and so also must seek refuge in the Absolutely All-Powerful One's high Presence. This One will close this world's door and open the one to the Hereafter, the world of wonders, and will replace this world with the next one so that we may rejoin the 99 percent of our friends who have left for the Intermediate World.

Given this, our true object of worship can only be the Majestic, All-Powerful One, the All-Merciful One of Infinite Beauty, the All-Wise One of Perfection, in Whose hand are the reins of all things, in Whose possession is the provision of every existence, Who sees everything and is omnipresent, unbounded by space, and free of any constraint, flaw, defect, or deficiency. As our unlimited need can be satisfied only by the One with Infinite Power and All-Encompassing Knowledge, He is the only One worthy of worship.

If you worship Him alone, you will attain a rank above all other creatures. If you do not, you will become a disgraced slave to impotent creation. If you rely upon your selfhood and power instead of prayer and trust in God, and claim an arrogant superiority, you will become lower than a bee or an ant and weaker than a fly or a spider with respect to positive acts and constructive invention. But your evil and destruction will weigh heavier than a mountain and be more harmful than a pestilence, for you have two aspects of being. One is positive and active and has to do with constructive invention, existence, and goodness; the other is negative and passive, and concerns destruction, nonexistence, and evil.

As for the first aspect of your being, you cannot compete with a bee or a sparrow, are weaker than a fly or a spider, and cannot achieve what they can. As for the second aspect, however, you can surpass mountains, Earth, and the heavens, for you can bear a burden that they cannot. Thus your acts have a wider impact than theirs. When you do something good or build something, it reaches only as far as your hand and strength. But your evil and destructive acts are aggressive and expandable.

For example, unbelief is an evil, an act of destruction, an absence of affirmation. It may look like a single sin, but it implies an insult to creation, the debasement of all Divine Names, and the degradation of humanity. Creation has a sublime rank and important task, for each part of it is a missive of the Lord, a mirror of His Glory, and a servant of His Divinity. Unbelief denies them the rank bestowed by these functions and reduces them to playthings of chance and insignificant, useless, and worthless objects doomed to decay and decomposition.

Unbelief insults the Divine Names, Whose beautiful inscriptions and manifestations are observed in the mirrors of all created forms throughout the universe. It also casts us down to a level more wretched and weak, helpless and destitute, than the lowliest animal. It reduces us to an ordinary, perishable billboard without meaning due to its inherent confusion and rapid decay. And this when humanity, in reality, is a poetic work of Wisdom that manifests all Divine Names; a great miracle of Power that, like a seed, contains the Tree of Creation; and God's vicegerent, superior to angels and higher than mountains, Earth, and heavens by virtue of the trust we have undertaken.

Let me sum this up. As regards evil and destruction, the soul (the evil-commanding self) may commit countless crimes and cause unlimited destruction, whereas its capacity to do good is limited. It can destroy a house within a day, but cannot rebuild it in 100 days. But if it abandons self-reliance and vanity and relies upon Divine aid to do good and constructive things, if it abandons evil and destruction and seeks Divine forgiveness and so becomes a perfect servant of God, it becomes the referent of: *God will change their evil deeds into good deeds* (27:50). That is, our infinite capacity for evil then is changed into an infinite ability for good. We attain the worth of "the best pattern of creation" and rise to the "highest of the high."

Consider then, O heedless one, the All-Mighty's Grace and Munificence. In reality, it is absolute justice to record one sin as 1,000 sins due to its consequences and effects, and a good act as only one. But God does the reverse: He records a sin as one and a good act as 10, 70, 700, or, in some cases, 7,000. From this we can understand that entering Hell is the result of one's deeds and pure justice, while entering Paradise is the result of His absolute Grace.

SECOND REMARK: Human beings have two faces. The first face looks to this worldly life because of our selfhood. Here we are poor creatures indeed. Human will is as feeble as a hair, human power is restricted to a most limited talent, human life is as short as a flash of light compared to the world's life, and our material existence is that of a tiny thing bound to decompose. In this state, we are no more than a feeble member of one species among countless others spread throughout the universe.

The second face looks to the eternal life because of our nature as God's servants. Our perception of helplessness and insufficiency as God's servants make us important, inclusive beings. The All-Wise Creator has implanted an infinite impotence and poverty in our nature so that each of us may be a comprehensive mirror reflecting the infinite manifestations of God's Compassion and Power, Richness and Generosity. Through belief and worship, therefore, we gain infinite power and limitless riches.

We resemble seeds, for each of us has the potential to engender and attain perfection. A seed is endowed by Power with great potential and is destined to put it into effect. According to Destiny's subtle program, it should germinate underground to grow into a "perfect" tree via its worship according to the language of its potential. If that seed abuses its potential to attract harmful substances, soon it will rot away in its narrow place. If it uses its potential properly, however, and in compliance with the laws of *Him Who splits the seed for sprouting* (6:95), it will emerge from its narrow place and grow into an awesome, fruitful tree. In addition, its tiny and particular nature will come to represent a great and universal truth.

Our essence also is equipped by Power with great potential and is inscribed by Destiny with important programs. If we use our potential and spiritual faculties in this narrow world under the soil of worldly life to satisfy the fancies of our carnal, evil-commanding selfhood, we will become corrupt, a rotten seed, for an insignificant pleasure during a short life. Thus we will depart from this world with a heavy spiritual burden on our unfortunate souls.

But if we germinate the seed of our potential under the "soil of worship" with the "water of Islam" and the "light of belief" according to the Qur'an's decrees, and if we use our spiritual faculties for their true purposes, we will grow into eternal, majestic trees whose branches extend into the Intermediate World and the world where our deeds take on the forms specific to the Hereafter. This will yield countless perfect fruits in the next world. We will become the fruit of the Tree of Creation, which will be favored in Paradise with infinite perfections and countless blessings.

We can make true progress only when we turn our faculties (e.g., intellect, heart, spirit, and imagination) to the eternal life, so that each will be occupied with its own kind of worship. What the misguided consider progress—subjecting our faculties to the carnal evil-commanding selfhood to taste all worldly pleasures—is nothing but decline and degradation. I once observed this truth in a vision, which is as follows:

I reached a huge city full of large palaces. Outside some of them, I noticed ongoing spectacles and shows to amuse and entertain. As I drew near to one of them, I saw that its owner was playing with a dog at the door. Women were chatting with young strangers, and girls were organizing children's games. The doorman was behaving as if he were their master. I realized that the palace was empty, with all important tasks left unattended, for its corrupted inhabitants were pursuing useless affairs.

I then came across another palace. A faithful dog was lying at the door, and beside it was a doorman with a stern, serious, and sober expression. The palace seemed so quiet that I entered in wonder and amazement. Inside was a scene of great activity, for the inhabitants were engaged in different, important tasks. The men on the first floor were managing the palace. On the second floor, girls and boys were studying. The women on the third floor were producing beautiful works of art and delicate embroidery. On the top floor, the owner was in constant communication with the king to secure his household's well-being and so that he could perform noble duties for his own progress and perfection. As they did not see me, I walked about unhindered.

Once outside, I saw that the city was full of similar palaces. When I asked about them, I was told that the palaces like the first one belonged to the foremost of the unbelievers and misguided, while those of the second type belonged to upright Muslim notables. In one corner, I came across a palace on which my name was written: "Said." As I looked at it closely, I felt as if I saw my image on it. Crying in bewilderment, I came to my senses and awoke.

I will now interpret this vision: The city is our social life and the terrain of human civilization. Each palace is a human being, and the inhabitants are human senses and faculties (e.g., eyes, ears, intellect, heart and spirit, and powers of anger and lust). Each sense and faculty has a particular duty of worship as well as particular pleasures and pains. The self and fancies, as well as the powers of anger and lust, correspond to the dog and the doorman. Thus, subjugating the sublime senses and faculties to carnal desires and fancies so that they forget their essential duties is decline and corruption. It certainly is not progress. You may interpret the other details for yourself.

THIRD REMARK: In our actions and bodily endeavors, we are like weak animals and helpless creatures. The realm at our disposal is so limited that our fingers can touch its circumference. Our weakness, impotence, and indolence are so great that even domesticated animals are influenced by them. If a domesticated animal is compared with its undomesticated counterpart, great differences can be seen.

But as passive, recipient beings who need to pray and petition, we are worthy travelers who are allowed to stay for a while in the guest-house of this world. We are guests of a Generous One, Who has put His infinite Compassion's treasuries at our disposal and subjugated His peerless works of creative power and special servants to us. Also, He has prepared for our use and pleasure such a vast arena that its radius is as far as sight or even imagination can reach.

If we rely on our physical and innate abilities, taking the worldly life as our goal and concentrating on its pleasures, we will suffocate within a very narrow circle. Furthermore, our bodily parts, senses, and faculties will bring suit and witness against us in the Hereafter. But if we know that we are guests and so spend our lives within the limits approved by our Generous Host, we will lead happy and peaceful lives and reach the highest rank. We will be rewarded with an everlasting life of bliss in the Hereafter, and all of our bodily members and faculties will testify in our favor.

Our wonderful faculties have not been given for use in this trivial worldly life; rather, they are for our eternal life. We have many more faculties and senses than animals do, but the pleasure we derive from our physical lives is much less than what animals derive. Every worldly pleasure bears traces of pain, and is spoiled with past sorrows, fears of the future, and pleasure's ultimate disappearance. Animals experience pleasure without pain, enjoyment without anxiety, and have no past sorrows or anxiety about the future. They enjoy comfortable lives and praise their Creator.

We have been created in the best pattern. If we concentrate on this worldly life we are far lower than a sparrow, although we have far more developed faculties than any animal. For example, a man gives his servant 10 gold coins and tells him to have a suit made for himself out of a certain cloth. He gives another servant 1,000 gold coins and sends him to the market with a shopping list. The former buys an excellent suit of the finest cloth. The latter acts foolishly, for he neither notices how much money he was given nor reads the shopping list. Thinking that he should imitate his friend, he goes to a shop and asks for a suit. The dishonest shopkeeper gives him a suit of the very worst-quality cloth. The unfortunate servant returns to his master and receives a severe reprimand and a terrible punishment. Anyone can see that the 1,000 gold coins were not given for a suit, but rather for a very important transaction.

In the same way, our spiritual faculties, feelings, and senses are much more developed than those of animals. For example, we can see all degrees of beauty, experience the particular tastes of all varieties of food, penetrate the many details of visible realities, yearn for all ranks of perfection, and so on. But animals, with the exception of a particular faculty that reaches a high state of development according to its particular duty, can realize only slight development, if any.

Our senses and feelings, which have developed a great deal owing to our mind and intellect, require that we have many faculties. Our many needs have caused us to evolve different types of feelings, to become very sensitive to many things. Also, due to our comprehensive nature we have been given desires turned to several aims and objectives. Our senses and faculties have greatly expanded due to the diversity of our essential duties. Furthermore, since we are inclined and able to worship, we have the potential to realize all kinds of perfection.

Such rich faculties and abundant potentialities cannot have been given to us for an insignificant, temporary, worldly life. In reality, they were given to us because our essential duty is to perceive our obligations, which are directed toward endless aims; to affirm our impotence, poverty, and insufficiency via worship; to study by our far-reaching sight and penetrating understanding; to bear witness to creation's glorification of God; to discern and be grateful for the All-Merciful One's aid sent in the form of bounties; and to gaze, reflect upon, and draw warnings from the miracles of His Power as manifested in creation.

O world-worshipping one charmed by the worldly life and ignorant of the meaning of your nature as the best pattern of creation! Once I saw the true nature of this worldly life in a vision, as follows: My Lord had caused me to set out on this journey. He gradually gave me some of the 60 gold coins He had allotted to me. This went on for some time, and after a while I arrived at an inn that provided some entertainment. I gambled away 10 gold coins in one night of entertainment and frivolity. The next morning, I had no money for the provisions I would need at my destination. All I had left was pain, sorrow, and regret left by sins and illicit pleasures. While I was in this wretched state, someone said to me: "You have lost all you had and deserve to be punished. Moreover, you will go on to your destination with no money. But if you use your mind, the door of repentance is not closed. When you receive the rest of the money, keep half in reserve and use it to buy what you will need at your destination."

My selfhood did not agree, so the man said: "Save a third of it then." Still my selfhood balked. The man insisted: "Then a quarter." I realized that my selfhood would be unable to abandon its addictions, so the man turned away indignantly and disappeared. At once, I found myself on a high-speed train traveling through a tunnel. I was alarmed, but there was no escape.

To my surprise, I saw very attractive flowers and tasty-looking fruits alongside the track, hanging out from the tunnels' sides. I foolishly attempted to pick some of them. But all around them were thorns that, because of the train's speed, tore my hands and made them bleed. Whatever I tried to hold onto slipped from my grasp. Suddenly an attendant came and said: "Give me 5 cents and I will give you as many flowers and fruits as you want. Otherwise, with your hands all cut up, you will lose a 100 instead of 5 cents. Also, you will be punished for picking them without permission."

Depressed by this condition, I looked out the window to see when the tunnel would end. But there was no end in sight. The tunnel's walls had many openings into which passengers were being thrown. Suddenly I caught sight of an opening just opposite me with a gravestone on either side. When I peered out, I made out my name, "Said," written in capital letters on a gravestone. I gave a cry of bewilderment and repentance. Unexpectedly, I heard the voice of the man who had advised me at the inn, asking: "Have you come to your senses?" I replied: "Yes, but I am in despair and there is nothing I can do." He told me to repent and trust in God, to which I replied that I would. Then I woke up and I found myself transformed into the New Said; the Old Said had gone away.

I will now interpret some aspects of this vision: The journey is our life, a journey from the incorporeal World of Eternity, passing through the stages of your mother's womb, youth, old age, the grave, the Intermediate World, Resurrection, and the Bridge. The 60 gold coins are the 60 years of an average lifetime. I was 45 when I had this vision. Only God knows when I will die. A sincere student of the Qur'an showed me the true path so that I might spend half of the remaining 15 years for the Hereafter.

The inn, I came to understand, was Istanbul. The train was time, and each wagon was a year. The tunnel was this worldly life. The thorny flowers and fruits were illicit pleasures and forbidden amusements that make the heart bleed with the idea of separation at the very moment you reach for them. Disappearance of pleasures increases sorrow, and besides, being unlawful, cause one to suffer punishment. The attendant had said: "Give me 5 cents, and I will give you as many flowers and fruits as you want." This means that the permissible tastes and pleasures, obtained in lawful ways, are enough to satisfy me and so there is no need to pursue illicit ways.

FOURTH REMARK: We resemble tender children. Our strength originates in our weakness, and our power in our impotence. This lack of strength and power has caused creation to be subjugated to us. Therefore if we perceive our weakness and become humble servants of God through our verbal and active prayers, and if we recognize our impotence and seek God's help, we will have shown our gratitude to Him for this subjugation of nature to us.

Moreover, God will enable us to reach our goal and achieve our aims in a way far beyond our own capability. Sometimes we wrongly attribute a wish's attainment to our own power and ability, when in reality it has been obtained for us through the prayer offered by the tongue of our disposition. Consider how great a source of power is a chick's weakness, for it causes the mother hen to attack even a lion. A lion cub's weakness subjugates a great lioness, which will suffer hunger to feed its baby. How remarkable is the powerful appeal inherent in weakness, and what a spectacular manifestation of Compassion for importunate beings.

In the same way, beloved children obtain their goals by weeping, wishing, or making sad faces, all of which can cause mighty people to serve them. If children rely on their own strength, in practical terms they can achieve nothing. Their weakness and powerlessness, as well as feelings of affection and protection, are so in their favor that a single gesture may allow them to subjugate powerful persons to themselves. But if they arrogantly deny the care and affection shown to them and claim to do all of this on their own, they deserve to be punished. Similarly, we deserve punishment if we deny our Creator's Mercy and show our ingratitude by saying that our own power and knowledge—not Divine Mercy—have achieved all of this. We will be like Korah, who said: *I have been given it (my possessions) on account of my knowledge* (28:78).

This shows that our observed dominion in nature, as well as our advancement and progress in civilization and technology, are mainly due to our essential weakness and helplessness, which attract Divine aid. Our poverty is the source of Divine provision, our ignorance is compensated for by Divine inspiration, and our need draws Divine favors. Divine Mercy, Affection, and Wisdom, not our own power and knowledge, have empowered us with dominion over creation and have put things at our disposal. Divine Authority and Compassion alone enable us, beings so weak that we can be defeated by a blind scorpion and a footless snake, to dress in silk produced by a worm and to eat the honey produced by a stinging insect.

Since this is the truth, O people, renounce arrogance and self-trust. Rather, affirm your impotence and weakness in God's high Presence by asking for His help and praying and entreating Him. Declare your poverty and insufficiency. Show that you are His true servant. Then say: *God is sufficient for us. Most sublime is He in Whom we trust* (3:173) and ascend to the higher ranks.

Do not say: "I am nothing. Why should the All-Wise Creator put creation at my disposal and demand universal gratitude?" In physical terms you are almost nothing, but your duty or rank makes you an attentive observer of this magnificent universe, an eloquent tongue of beings declaring Divine Wisdom, a perceptive student of this Book of Creation, an admiring overseer of the creatures glorifying God's praise, a respected master of worshipping beings.

You are, O humanity, an insignificant particle, a poor creature and weak animal in terms of your physical being and soul. And so you are being carried away by creation's huge waves. But if you are perfected through the light of belief, which comprises the radiance of Divine love, and through the training of Islam, you will find a kingliness in your being a servant, a comprehensiveness in your particularity, a world in your small entity, and a very high rank in your insignificance. The realm of your supervision of the rest of creation will be so broad that you can say: "My Compassionate Lord has made the world a home for me. He has given me the sun and moon as lamps, spring as a bunch of roses, summer as a banquet of favors, and animals as obedient servants. He has put plants and vegetation at my disposal, as ornaments and provisions to my home."

In conclusion, if you obey your evil-commanding selfhood and Satan, you will fall to the lowest depth. But if you follow the truth and the Qur'an, you will ascend to the highest rank and become the most excellent pattern of creation.

FIFTH REMARK: We have been sent here as guests with a special responsibility. Endowed with important potentials, we have been assigned important duties and strongly urged to carry them out. If we do not, we will be punished. To make the mystery of "being the best pattern of creation" more comprehensible, I will summarize the essentials of worship and duties.

Our worship consists of two aspects. The first aspect is implicit and concerns reflection and consciousness. It involves our submitting to the Sovereignty of His Lordship over creation and observing in amazement the works of His Beauty and Perfection. We draw the attention of others to the intricate, ornamented works of art: the sacred Divine Names' manifestations. We also measure in "units" of due perception and discernment the gems of the Lord's Names, each of which is a hidden spiritual treasure, and evaluate them with our hearts' grateful appreciation.

Then we study the pages of creation and the sheets of the heavens and Earth, each of which is a missive of Divine Power, and contemplate them in great admiration. Afterwards, as we gaze in amazement and admiration upon the subtle ornamentation and refined skills seen in creation, we ardently desire to know their Beautiful Creator and yearn to enter His Presence, where we hope to be received into His favor.

The second aspect, visible prayer, means turning toward our Majestic Creator, Who wills Himself to be known through His artistry's miracles. Supplicating directly in His presence, we unburden ourselves to Him in sincere belief and try to acquire knowledge of Him. We discern that a Compassionate Lord wants to be loved through His Compassion's beautiful fruits, and so make ourselves loved by Him through devoting our love and adoration to Him.

Seeing that the Generous Provider nourishes us with the best and dearest of His material and spiritual favors, we respond with gratitude and praise, expressed through our works, deeds, lifestyle and, if possible, our senses and faculties. Observing that a Lord of Beauty and Majesty manifests Himself in the mirror of beings and draws attention to His Glory and Perfection, Majesty and Beauty, we respond: "God is the Greatest. Glory be to God," and prostrate before Him in wonder and adoration.

Noticing that the One of Absolute Riches displays His limitless wealth and treasuries in an infinitely generous fashion, we respond by glorifying and praising Him and, displaying our need, ask Him for His favors. Observing that the Majestic Creator has arranged Earth like an exhibition to display His matchless works, we appreciate them by saying: "What wonders God has willed and created," confirm their beauty by saying: "God bless them," show our wonder by saying: "Glory be to God," and express our admiration by saying: "God is the Greatest."

We see that the Unique One shows His Oneness throughout creation by His particular signs and specific decrees, and by His inimitable stamps and seals that He has put on each creature. He inscribes signs of His Oneness on everything and raises the flag of His Unity throughout the world to proclaim His Lordship. We respond to this with belief, affirmation, admission, and with testimony to His Unity, devotion, and sincere worship.

We may attain true humanity through such types of worship and reflection. We may demonstrate that we are the best pattern of creation and, by the grace of belief, become trustworthy vicegerents of God on Earth.

CHAPTER 4

How Western Philosophies and the Qur'an View History

HOW WESTERN PHILOSOPHIES AND
THE QUR'AN VIEW HISTORY

WESTERN PHILOSOPHIES OF HISTORY AND
THE CONCEPT OF HISTORY IN THE QUR'AN

Could there be a political purpose behind some of the West's recent philosophies? Before labeling me "unscientific" or a "skeptic," remember that those people who have made gigantic advances in science and technology also posited such theories as biological evolution, the (white) European male's brain composition as biologically suitable for science, the Eastern [Muslim] brain for romanticism, and the (black) African brain for jazz and athleticism.

Darwin and Scientific Proof

Almost all nineteenth-century Western philosophical theories were based on the ideas of progress and evolution. At its roots, Darwin's theory of evolution is derived from Malthusian population theories. Malthus,[1] an Anglican priest interested in how demographic factors influenced economics, argued that only producers have a right to survive, while non-producers (e.g., the poor, sick, disabled, and so on) are condemned by nature to be eliminated. Darwin,[2] a great admirer of this socioeconomic theory, developed the "scientific" theory that selection is a law encompassing all of nature. According to it, the powerful survive and the weak are cleared away over time.

Referring to P.-P. Grassé, a contemporary French zoologist, Maurice Bucaille says that Darwin's work contains no scientific proof, although Darwin made plenty of observations to support his theory, and that his theory is more philosophical than scientific.[3] Thus, if there are some socioeconomic worries related to a "scientific" theory that has shaken science for the last two centuries and has been used as a weapon against religion, why should there not be a political purpose behind some philosophical theories?

Although unable to affirm this completely in such a short article, Western philosophies of history, especially those of the nineteenth century, clearly had underlying political intentions and functioned as ideological precepts for Western colonialism. Almost all of these philosophies suggested that humanity was flowing irreversibly toward good, that the flow could not be stopped, and that such forward movement or progress was continuous. For instance, Spencer's sociology is a continuation of Darwin's theory. Comte actually wrote that humanity, having passed through the stages of religion and metaphysics, is now in the last and happiest age of progress: the stage of science. We find the same understanding of progress in the historical philosophies of Herder, Fichte, Hegel, and Marx.

Western Philosophies of History

According to Siddiqi, Hegel's philosophy of history can be defined as a composition of conflicts and contradictions, for Hegel holds that each period in the history of social civilization represents an independent unity.[4] This unity, which is thoroughly its own, gradually gives rise to its antithesis and results in a thesis–antithesis conflict. After a while, the sides agree on a synthesis that encompasses both the original thesis and antithesis and engenders a new thesis. The process then begins again. This tripartite system causes thought to progress until it attains to *Geist*.

Hegel, seemingly under the influence of Indian philosophies, asserted that *Geist* is the universal spirit manifesting itself through concrete events. Each event, together with its accompanying philosophy, is a stage in this spirit's evolutionary course. Thus no philosophy can be considered wrong. Every event is planned by an absolute, determining will, and all desires, inclinations, efforts, and conflicts are means that *Geist* uses to attain self-realization. Therefore everything happens irrespectively or independently of our free will, and we are reduced to the status of an all-powerful will's plaything. Given this scenario, only those who perceive this will's demands or (more clearly) the course of events and act accordingly are the heroes of their time who must be obeyed absolutely.

Basing his theory mainly on Feurbach's atheism, Darwin's evolutionist theory, and Hegel's dialectics, Marx stated that he "stood the Hegelian man who stands on his head, upright on his feet." (To this, an Egyptian Muslim thinker responds: "Is man really a being who 'walks' on his head?") All of Marx's philosophical, historical, sociological, or economic theories posit the idea that men and women are beings who "walk on their feet"—in other words, beings whose minds are commanded by their feet.

Marx maintains that humanity is an outcome of the legal relationships between people and the tools of production that we found in nature and developed over time. What we call human thought is the reflection in our mind of the relations between ourselves, our material and economic lives, and the tools of production. Given this, Marx essentially states that true knowledge is produced in the mind only when the legal relationships between people and the tools of production are established in a communist system according to the principles of communism.

Such a conclusion shows that Marxism is substantially false, because Marx conceived of it within a capitalistic system. Marx viewed human life or history as an unending economic-based conflict between individuals, classes, and people. As this inevitable conflict will produce communism after passing through the primitive, feudal and capitalistic stages, these stages cannot be criticized, because humanity is naturally and intrinsically bound to pass through them.

As for the once-widespread theory of historicism, we cannot find a suitably long and stable period of human history from which to derive any long-term general rules, because sociological laws vary according to time and place[5] and history never repeats itself at the same level. We cannot predict anything with certainty, for the relationships between events are very complex.

Historicism, however, places great importance on human activity, even though nothing that we can conceive of can be realized unless it conforms to history's main course, which depends on certain blind and irresistible laws. Humanity only acts reasonably when it acts in accordance with these independent laws and the urgent, inevitable changes they impose. Given this, people are to lend a hand to the changes or attempts that they are expected to accept, because any desire to give a better shape to the world is unreasonable.

A Criticism

In sum, these philosophies of history state that:

- Humanity is progressing continually toward the final happy end.
- This progress depends on history's fatalistic and irresistible laws, all of which are completely independent of us. Our only option is to obey them, for if we do not we will be eliminated.
- All stages (e.g., primitive, feudal, or capitalistic) through which we inevitably pass should not be criticized, for we have no choice but to pass through them.

Such philosophies of history imply that the present socio-economic and even political conditions are inevitable, because they were dictated by nature, which decrees the survival of the most powerful. If this reality favors the West, communities that choose to survive must concede to Western dominion.

How can we agree with this, given that we clearly see that any age contains other ages? Consider the following points:

- Some people live in the Electronic Age while others, for all practical purposes, are still in the Middle Ages or even the Stone Age. Thus it is more logical to say that history is cyclical instead of linear, and that we make history through our free choice instead of being at the mercy of some nominal laws without real existence.

- Morality, science, and history cannot approve of injustice in any form or case.
- Why do those who support such theories prefer to maintain the domination of Christianity, despite the vast and rapid spread of Islam at its expense, if history's fatalistic laws apparently have sided with Islam?

Like every other incoherent and false philosophy, these philosophies did not last long. By the twentieth century, atomic physics had dethroned mechanical physics, a development that made all gross materialistic and positivistic worldviews, as well as evolutionist conceptions of history, obsolete. Such theories and ideas were replaced by philosophies of history that sought to secure the West's future and did not place absolute confidence in science and technology.

According to Danilevsky's[6] philosophy of history, a civilization is not transformed into another and thus each one will die. A civilization is a culture's further step, and each culture develops one or more of humanity's values. Contemporary Western civilization is based on science. No civilization can claim total superiority over all others, and a people that has reached the stage of civilization is doomed to collapse after a long decline. Thus Western civilization one day will become a thing of the past.

Spengler, whose *The Decline of the West* shook the West in the early twentieth century, wrote that there are many cultures and that each great culture is unique. He agreed with Danilevsky that none of them can claim total superiority over the others. A civilization manifests itself in large cities as the inevitable result of culture. Over time, the desire for living dies away and women no longer bear children. Belief is replaced by scientific irreligion or dull metaphysics. Any civilization entering this stage either gives birth to materialism, greed, a passion for power and/or sex, and class conflict, or results in imperialism and finally collapses. Spengler holds that contemporary Western civilization, with all its large cities, railways, and skyscrapers, will in the near future become an ethnographic museum.

Toynbee's[7] ideas can be traced in the Muslim historian Ibn Khaldun,[8] often called the "father" of historiography. Toynbee maintains that civilization is the work of a creative minority in a propitious clime that begins to decay as the founding minority loses its energy and ability to deal with new situations.

According to Ibn Khaldun, who to some extent influenced many twentieth-century philosophers, civilization (*'umran*) is based on tribal solidarity, the distinguishing mark of nomadic life. Nomads lead a very simple life and know nothing of luxury (as understood in the urban sense). He also held that people feel an intrinsic need to live together and that such togetherness requires sanctions to control aggressive people. These sanctions either are established by a powerful individual or determined naturally by tribal solidarity. Thus the need for a common authority results in state formation.

Ibn Khaldun also claims that social solidarity is much stronger in nomadic tribes and, if united with religion, becomes an irresistible power. But as the state becomes more firmly established, social solidarity is no longer needed and a sedentary lifestyle allows people to indulge in luxury, which dissolves solidarity. The ruler, trying to strengthen his authority, forms a council and a troop of royal guards. But nothing keeps the state or civilization from collapse: Increasing extravagance, luxury, indulgence of every kind, and heavy taxes bring about its ruin.

The Qur'anic Concept of History

The Qur'anic concept of history differs markedly from those discussed earlier. First, it views history from the perspective of unchanging principles, while philosophers of history or sociologists interpret past events and present situations to build their theories. Second, contrary to the fatalism of all other philosophies, including even Ibn Khaldun's, the Qur'an stresses the individual's free choice and moral conduct. Although Divine Will, emphasized in the Qur'an, could be regarded in some respects as the counterpart of Hegel's *Geist* or as other philosophies' absolute and irresistible laws of history, the Qur'an never denies human free will.

According to the Qur'an, God tests us in this life. We are the ones who sow the field of this world and harvest it in the next (and eternal) life. Given this, the stream of events is that which God causes us to undergo so that we may learn how to distinguish good from evil. Testing requires that the one being tested be free to choose between allowed and prohibited, good and bad—in other words, to have free will. And so history is made up of our own choices and not laid out by a compelling Divine Will. God has made our ability to choose the sole condition for the activation of His universal Will. When this point is understood, the groundless nature of Western philosophies of history, especially with respect to their conception of an "inevitable end," is quite clear.

QUESTION: If civilizations are not essentially subject to an inevitable end, why could no past civilization resist decadence and time's corrosive power?

ANSWER: Now we have come to the core of the issue. Ibn Khaldun, Toynbee, Spengler, and other philosophers of history formed a mistaken conception of history because they did not try to discover the real dynamics of historical movements. Rather, they sought to explain the apparent causes behind a civilization's establishment, flourishing, and decay. Whoever looks to the past will arrive at the same conclusions. But just because no community has remained at its peak does not mean that this is an inevitable end or a determinist grip on each nation's fate. Past civilizations collapsed because they did not heed the warnings of what had happened to earlier peoples. Accepting historical determinism causes us to nullify free will and consider the warnings and advice found in the Divine Scriptures and social sciences as useless and absurd.

Since humanity is sent here to be tested, each person must have a carnal self that serves as the source of all our desires and animal appetites. In addition, we have a natural inclination to live with other people and have a complex relationship with our natural environment. Thus our carnal desires should be limited and our relations with our human and natural environments based on justice, as such a situation will allow us to live in peace with ourselves, our environment, and nature.

Nevertheless, history shows those who cannot control their carnal desires may try to dominate others because they are not satisfied with their share in society. If they realize their ambitions, they may seek to justify their actions by promulgating a constitution to govern the people. It is always easy to make people "vote" for a constitution.

This is what happens when Divine laws are abrogated. When people sincerely believe in One God as Lord, Sovereign, and Master, without any intermediary class or clergy, and when they are really conscious of the meaning of Divine Unity, something wonderful happens. Being delivered from their humiliating slavery to carnal desires, worldly positions or other beings, and eradicating false and artificial contradictions (e.g., black vs. white, clergy vs. laity, ruler vs. ruled, employer vs. employed), people are elevated so high that they become servants of One God, and no one attempts to dominate others through money, color, race, or weapons.

According to the Qur'an, all people are creatures of One God and therefore equal in His sight. Furthermore, we lack the knowledge and power to establish the rules that will allow the majority of people to live at peace with themselves, other people, and the natural environment. Above all, we must be at peace with our Creator and Sustainer. Given this, only God has exclusive sovereignty in the heavens and on Earth.

God asks us, as we can deduce from our own reasoning, to build our worldly existence on three foundations: justice, religious– moral values, and the Divine laws of life and nature. The

Qur'an invites us, first of all, to believe in and worship One God so that we may lead a balanced life, which it defines as attaining true inward happiness and peace, coexisting with other people in accordance with the rules of justice, and avoiding being led astray by our carnal evil-commanding self.

Second, the Qur'an lays down some moral–legal, principles, such as:

> Give your relatives their due, and also the poor and the wayfarer. Do not spend wastefully, in the manner of a spendthrift.... Do not kill your children for fear of poverty, for We provide for them and for you. Avoid unlawful sexual intercourse. Do not kill anyone which God has forbidden, except for just cause. Do not come near the orphan's property, except to improve it. Fulfill covenants, give full measure when you measure, and weigh with the balance that is right. (17:26, 31-35)

The Qur'an prohibits usury, black-marketeering, hoarding, theft, gambling, cheating, and other social ills. It orders us to study nature, discover its laws, and make progress in science. It also discusses vital principles that are part of our "fate," such as the truths that patience and forbearance usually bring success and victory, and that working produces wealth while inertia and laziness cause poverty.

According to the Qur'an, we determine our own future through our own free will by either obeying or ignoring justice, religious–moral values, and the Divine laws of nature. If at least a majority of a community obeys God and His religious and natural laws, nothing will prevent its inhabitants from realizing individual and social peace, happiness, and harmony. Without this obedience, even the most glittering community will decay.

Also, it must be emphasized that the Qur'an does not accept an inevitable end for any civilization. It can remain at its peak as long as it follows the right way. The fact that no civilization has yet done so does not mean that it is impossible. For history is cyclical but not linear, any civilization that is on the brink of collapse because of its deviation from the correct path can be saved and even rise again if it reforms itself. In brief:

- God revealed Islam through all of the Prophets, who called their people to the same essentials of belief, to worship only One God, and to pursue virtue and abandon vice. The differences seen among the revealed religions lie in secondary matters, such as those connected with then-existing economic and political relationships.

- As the Qur'an, the universe, and humanity are three manifestations of one truth, there are no contradictions or incompatibilities between religion (Qur'anic truths) and science (truths derived from the objective study of the universe). True belief is not based on blind imitation; rather, it appeals to the reason and the heart in order to combine reason's affirmation and the heart's inner experience and submission.

- Nothing is more effective against the cynical use of power than serious and sincere religious belief. Therefore it is not surprising that secular political opinion-makers attack or mock religion, particularly Islam, by claiming that religion inspires killing. Such claims are no more than attempts to disguise the real cause behind the millions of deaths engendered by colonialism, two world wars, various undeclared wars, and communism.

- Cartesian dualism, although developed to defend religion against science, gave science superiority over religion and primacy in practical life and thought. As a result, religion was restricted to blind belief beyond the reach of research, verification, and reasoning. It also became totally irrelevant to the world and worldly life.

- True humanity lies in restricting our negative aspects and channeling them into virtue, and in acquiring good qualities so that we may become good, worshipful servants of God and useful members of society.

- History is the result of human choice and not of a compelling will. God allows the stream of events—history—to unfold so that good may be distinguished from evil.

NOTES

INTRODUCTION

1   The Ottoman State existed from 1299 to 1922. It reached its zenith during the reigns of Mehmet I the Conqueror (1451-1481), Bayezid II (1481-1512), Selim I (1512-20), and Suleyman I [the Magnificent] (1520-66). Mustafa Kemal proclaimed the Republic of Turkey in Anatolia, the defeated Ottoman Empire's heartland, on October 29, 1923. (Ed.)

2   The Sunna is the record of the Messenger's every act, word, and confirmation, as well as the second source of Islamic legislation and life (the Qur'an is the first one). In addition to establishing new principles and rules, the Sunna clarifies the ambiguities in the Qur'an by expanding upon what is mentioned only briefly in it, specifies what is unconditional, and enables generalizations from what is specifically stated and particularizations from what is generally stated.

CHAPTER I
PRELIMINARY ARTICLES

1   God has three kinds of Attributes: Essential Attributes (e.g., Existence, Having No Beginning, Eternal Permanence, Being Unlike the Created, Self-Subsistence, and Absolute Oneness); Positive Attributes (e.g., Life, Knowledge, Power, Speech, Will, Hearing, Seeing, and Creating); and innumerable "Negative" Attributes, summed up in the phrase "God is absolutely free from any defect and shortcoming." The Attributes are the sources of the Names: Life gives rise to the All-Living, Knowledge to the All-Knowing, Power to the All-Powerful. About 1,000 of God's many Names are known to us. The Names are the sources of the acts: giving life has its source in the All-Living, and knowing everything down to the smallest things originates in the All-Knowing. God is "known" by His acts, Names, and Attributes. Whatever exists in the universe's material and immaterial worlds is the result of the Names' and Attributes' manifestations. For example, universal and individual provision points to His Name the All-Providing, the All-Healing is the source of medicine and patient recovery, true philosophy has its source in Wisdom, and so on. The acts, Names, and Attributes are the "links" between God and the created, or the "reflectors" by which people can acquire knowledge of God. The principles of belief consist of belief in God's Existence and Unity, Resurrection and afterlife, Prophethood and all Prophets, the Divine Book, angels, and Divine Destiny (including human free will), and such other things as Divine Justice with its dimensions of unity, gathering, destiny, forgiveness, munificence, and mercy.

2   Being the final and unaltered Divine Revelation to humanity, the Qur'an is valid for all times, places, and people.

3   Islam teaches that no Prophet or Messenger will come after Prophet Muhammad, and that Islam is the final and perfect religion for all times and all people.

⁴ Albert Einstein (1879-1955): German-American physicist who developed the special and general theories of relativity and won the Nobel Prize for Physics in 1921 for his explanation of the photoelectric effect. (Ed.)

⁵ Galileo (1564-1642): Italian natural philosopher, astronomer, and mathematician who made fundamental contributions to the sciences of motion, astronomy, and strength of materials, and to the development of the scientific method. (Ed.)

⁶ Johann Wolfgang von Goethe (1749-1832): German poet, novelist, playwright, and natural philosopher, the greatest figure of the German Romantic period and of German literature as a whole. (Ed.)

⁷ Tomáš Garrigue Masaryk (1850-1937): Chief founder and first president (1918-35) of Czechoslovakia, and a philosopher by training. (Ed.)

⁸ Bertrand Russell (1872-1970): English logician and philosopher, best known for his work in mathematical logic and his social and political campaigns, including his advocacy of pacifism and nuclear disarmament. He received the Nobel Prize for Literature in 1950. (Ed.)

⁹ Sir Isaac Newton (1642/3-1727): English physicist and mathematician, the culminating figure of the seventeenth century's scientific revolution. In mechanics, his three laws of motion, the basic principles of modern physics, resulted in the formulation of the law of universal gravitation. (Ed.)

¹⁰ In any publication dealing with Prophet Muhammad, his name or title is followed by the phrase "upon him be peace and blessings," to show our respect for him and because it is a religious requirement to do so. A similar phrase is used for his Companions and other illustrious Muslims: "May God be pleased with him (or her)." However, as this practice might be distracting to non-Muslim readers, these phrases do not appear in this book, on the understanding that they are assumed and that no disrespect is intended. (Ed.)

¹¹ St. Paul (10?-67?): First-century Jew who, after first being a bitter enemy of Christianity, later became an important figure in its history. [Although he never met Jesus or heard him teach], he became the leading Apostle (missionary) of the new movement and played a decisive part in extending it beyond the limits of Judaism to become a worldwide religion. (Ed.)

¹² Sir James George Frazer (1854-1941): British anthropologist, folklorist, and classical scholar. His distinction between magic (an attempt to control events by technical acts based upon faulty reasoning) and religion (an appeal for help to spiritual beings) has been basically assumed in much anthropological writing. His evolutionary sequence of magical, religious, and scientific thought is no longer accepted. (Ed.)

¹³ Sir Edward Taylor (1832-1917): Coined the term *animism* (a belief in individual souls or *anima* in all things, even trees and mountains), which he posited as the first stage of religious evolution. (Ed.)

¹⁴ Wilhelm Schmidt (1868-1954): German anthropologist and Roman Catholic priest who led the influential cultural-historical European school of ethnology. He maintained that most primitive peoples believed in a Supreme Being and that their religions might correctly be regarded as monotheistic. (Ed.)

[15] Jalal al-Din al-Rumi (1207-73): The greatest Sufi master and poet in Persian; famous for his lyrics and for his didactic epic *Masnawi-i Ma'nawi* (Spiritual Couplets), which widely influenced Muslim Sufi thought and literature. (Ed.)

[16] Emile Durkheim (1858-1917): French social scientist who developed a vigorous methodology combining empirical research with sociological theory, considered the founder of the French school of sociology; Max Weber (1864-1920): German sociologist and political economist known for his thesis of the "Protestant Ethic," relating Protestantism to capitalism, and for his ideas on bureaucracy. (Ed.)

[17] William James (1842-1910): American philosopher and psychologist who developed the philosophy of pragmatism, a philosophical movement that has had a major impact on American culture since the late 19th century. Pragmatism calls for ideas and theories to be tested in practice, by assessing whether acting upon the idea or theory produces desirable or undesirable results. Pragmatists call for testing all claims about truth, knowledge, morality, and politics in this way. (Ed.)

[18] Sigmund Freud (1856-1939): Austrian neurologist and founder of psychoanalysis, which is simultaneously a theory of the human psyche, a therapy for relieving its ills, and an optic for interpreting culture and society. (Ed.)

[19] Ludwig (Andreas) Feuerbach (1804-72): German philosopher and moralist remembered for his influence on Karl Marx and his humanistic theologizing. (Ed.)

[20] Karl Marx (1818-83): Sociologist, historian, and economist. He published (with Friedrich Engels) *The Communist Manifesto* and *Das Kapital*. These writings and others by Marx and Engels form the basis of Marxism. (Ed.)

[21] Auguste Comte (1798-1857): French philosopher known as the founder of sociology and positivism. Comte gave the science of sociology its name and established the new subject in a systematic fashion. (Ed.)

[22] Ferdinand-Édouard Buisson (1841-1932): French educator who reorganized France's primary school system. Appointed inspector general of the Paris public schools (1871), he had to resign for urging the elimination of religious instruction. As national director of elementary education (1879-96), he helped Premier Jules Ferry draft statutes that took the public schools out of church control (1881, 1886) and made primary education free and compulsory (1882). (Ed.)

[23] Georg Wilhelm Friedrich Hegel (1770-1831): German philosopher who developed a dialectical scheme emphasizing the progress of history and ideas from thesis to antithesis to synthesis. (Ed.)

[24] Benedetto Croce (1866-1952): Historian, humanist, and foremost Italian philosopher of the first half of the twentieth century. (Ed.)

[25] Immanuel Kant (1724-1804): German philosopher whose comprehensive and systematic work in the theory of knowledge, ethics, and aesthetics greatly influenced all subsequent philosophy, especially Kantianism and Idealism. (Ed.)

[26] Friedrich Schleiermacher (1768-1834): German theologian, preacher, and classical philologist, generally recognized as the founder of modern Protestant theology. (Ed.)

[27] Erich Fromm (1900-80): German-born U.S. psychoanalyst and social philosopher who explored the interaction between psychology and society. He believed that applying psy-

choanalytic principles to cure cultural ills would allow humanity to develop a psychologically balanced "sane society." (Ed.)

28 Oswald Spengler (1880-1936): German philosopher who claimed that since most civilizations must pass through a life cycle, historians can reconstruct the past and predict "the spiritual forms, duration, rhythm, meaning and product of the still unaccomplished stages of our Western history." (Ed.)

29 René Guénon (1886-1951): French student of traditional wisdom who conducted research in Greek, Latin, English, Italian, German, Spanish, Sanskrit, Hebrew, Arabic, and various Chinese languages; Alexis Carrel (1873-1944): French surgeon who received the 1912 Nobel Prize for Physiology or Medicine for developing a method of suturing blood vessels; Max Planck (1858-1947): German theoretical physicist who originated quantum theory, which won him the Nobel Prize for Physics in 1918. This theory revolutionized our understanding of atomic and subatomic processes; Boris Pasternak (1890-1960): Russian poet whose novel *Doctor Zhivago*, an epic of wandering, spiritual isolation, and love amid the harshness of the Russian Revolution and its aftermath, helped win him the Nobel Prize for Literature in 1958 (declined). James Jeans (1877-1946): British astronomer who proposed a tidal theory based on a star passing close to the sun and pulling matter out which condensed into the planets. He also worked on thermodynamics, heat, and other aspects of radiation. (Ed.)

30 For a detailed analysis of these characteristics in relation to Prophet Muhammad, refer to M. Fethullah Gülen, *The Messenger of God Muhammad*, The Light, Inc., NJ: 2005, chapters 2-4. (Ed.)

31 Said Nursi (1876-1960): One of the greatest contemporary Muslim scholars; often credited with preserving Islam in Turkey during a time of enforced secularization and official hostility toward any personal or social display of Islam. (Ed.)

32 Said Nursi, *The Letters* (Turkey: The Light, 2002), 2:1-2.

33 Said Nursi, *The Words*, vol. 1 (Turkey: The Light, 2002).

34 Quoted from *The Words* by Said Nursi (Eighth Word).

35 God declares in the Qur'an: *I shall not allow to go to waste the deed of any doer among you, whether be a male or female: you are one from the other* (3:195). It is clear that Islam does not discriminate between men and women in religious responsibility. Each gender shares most of the responsibilities, but each one has certain responsibilities that are particular to it. The Qur'an usually uses the masculine form of address, for this is one of Arabic's characteristics. In almost every language, the masculine form is used for a group comprising both men and women, like the English word *mankind*, which includes both men and women. So, *brotherhood* also includes sisterhood, and, since the believers comprise both male and female believers, the believers are bothers and sisters. However, in order to maintain the original text and avoid repetition, usually we do not mention the feminine forms in translation.

36 *Hadith Qudsi*: This is a specific category of sayings from the Prophet. The wording is the Prophet's, but the meaning belongs to God.

37 The tree with various fruits shows the seal of Divinity, Whose unique virtue is "to create everything out of one thing" and "to change everything into one thing," to make various plants and fruits from the same soil, to create all living things from one drop

of water, and to nourish and sustain all living things in the same manner but through different foods.

38 The first ecumenical council of the Christian church, met in Nicaea (now Iznik, Turkey) in 325. It was called by Emperor Constantine I, an unbaptized catechumen (neophyte), who presided over the opening session and took part in the discussions. He hoped that a general church council would defeat Arianism, an Eastern creed proposed by Arius of Alexandria, that Christ is not divine but a created being. The council condemned Arius and, with some reluctance, incorporated the nonscriptural word *homoousios* ("of one substance") into the Nicene Creed to signify that the Son has absolute equality with the Father. The emperor then exiled Arius, an act that, while manifesting a solidarity of church and state, underscored the importance of secular patronage in ecclesiastical affairs. (Ed.)

39 Original Sin: The Christian doctrine that humanity was born sinful because of Adam's and Eve's sin in the Garden of Eden, and that Jesus Christ had to sacrifice his life to wipe out this sin and thereby secure a person's entrance to heaven. This and other doctrines, as well as Christianity's early history, are documented in such books as Will Durant's *Caesar and Christ*, Bruce Metzger's *The Canon of the New Testament: Its Origin, Development, and Significance*, W. H. C. Frend's *Rise of Christianity*, and Richard E. Rubenstein's *When Jesus Became God*. (Ed.)

40 The Battle of Badr: Fought in 624, it was the Muslims' first military victory: 314 Muslims defeated 950 polytheists. This battle seriously damaged Makkan prestige, strengthened the Muslims' position in Madina, and established Islam as a viable force in the Arabian peninsula. (Ed.)

41 The Companions: According to Ibn Hajar al-Asqalani (*Al-Isaba*, 1:7), scholars define a Companion as "a believer who saw and heard the Messenger at least once and died as a believer." Even though some scholars have stipulated that a "potential" Companion should have lived in the Messenger's company for one or even two years, most scholars say it is enough to have been present in his radiant atmosphere long enough to derive some benefit. (Ed.)

42 Abu Bakr (c.573-634; reigned 632-34): the Prophet's closest companion and adviser, and successor to his administrative functions as caliph. In Madina he was the Prophet's chief adviser (622-32) and entrusted with conducting the pilgrimage (631) and leading the public prayers in Madina during the Prophet's last illness. (Ed.)

43 'Umar Ibn al-Khattab (586-644; reigned 634-44): The second Muslim caliph, under whom Muslim armies conquered Mesopotamia and Syria and began the conquest of Iran and Egypt. A strong ruler, stern toward offenders, and ascetic to the point of harshness, he was universally respected for his justice and authority. (Ed.)

44 There is an important point to be added in this connection. When a Prophet passed away, over time his nation altered some principles of his religion, borrowed polytheistic elements from pagan practices, and went astray, thus corrupting the Divine religion. This is one of the reasons for the Prophets being sent one after the other.

45 The best-known Books of Tradition are those compiled by Bukhari (d. 870), Muslim (d. 875), Abu Dawud (d. 888), Tirmidhi (d. 892), Ibn Maja (d. 886), and al-Nasa'i (d. 915). (Ed.)

[46]   George Orwell, *Animal Farm* (Middlesex, UK: Penguin, 1957), 114.

[47]   *Time*, "Killing for God," (4 Dec. 1995), vol. 146, no. 23. Reported by Johanna McGeary and Eric Silver/Jerusalem and John Moody/New York with other bureaus.

[48]   Muhammad Asad, *Islam at the Crossroads* (New Era Publications: 1982), 5.

[49]   'Ali Ibn Abu Talib (c.600-661, reigned 656-61): The Prophet's son-in-law and fourth caliph. The question of his right to rule resulted in the only major split in Islam (into Sunni and Shi'ah branches). He is revered by the Shi'ah as the only true successor to the Prophet. (Ed.)

CHAPTER 2
ISLAM AND SCIENCE

[1]   Quoted by A. Karim in *Islam's Contribution to Science and Civilization*.

[2]   *Pakistan Quarterly*, vol. 4, no. 3.

[3]   For these quotations, see Abul A'la al-Mawdudi, *Towards Understanding Islam* (Kuwait: IIFSO, 1970), 69-70, footnote 1.

[4]   Abul-Fazl Ezzati, *An Introduction to the History of the Spread of Islam* (London: 1978), 378.

[5]   Sir Thomas Arnold and Alfred Guillaume (eds.), *The Legacy of Islam* (Oxford, UK: Clarendon, 1931 [1947]), 9.

[6]   *Indiculus Luminosus*, trans. by Dozy and quoted by Ezzati, *Introduction*, 98-99.

[7]   Quoted by Ezzati, *Introduction*, 235-37.

[8]   Said Nursi, "Epigrams," *The Letters*, Vol. 2 (London: Truestar, 1995).

[9]   David Hume (1711-76): Scottish philosopher, historian, economist, and essayist, known especially for his philosophical empiricism and skepticism. He believed that no theory of reality is possible and that there can be no knowledge of anything beyond experience. (Ed.)

[10] Sir Karl Popper (1902-94): Austrian-born British philosopher of natural and social science who subscribed to antideterminist metaphysics, believing that knowledge evolves from the mind's experience. (Ed.)

[11] René Guénon, *Orient et Occident* (Istanbul: 1980), 57. Turkish trans. by F. Arslan.

[12] This occurred under Emperor Constantine (280?-337), the first Roman emperor to profess Christianity (312). He started the empire's evolution into a Christian state, and provided the impulse for a distinctively Christian culture that prepared the way for the growth of the Byzantine and Western medieval cultures. (Ed.)

[13] Roger Bacon (c.1220-92): English Franciscan philosopher, educational reformer, and a major medieval proponent of experimental science. (Ed.)

[14] St. Thomas Aquinas (1224/25-74): Italian Dominican theologian, the foremost medieval Scholasticist. Although many modern Roman Catholic theologians do not find St. Thomas altogether congenial, he is nevertheless recognized by the Roman Catholic Church as its foremost Western philosopher and theologian. (Ed.)

[15] Nicholas de Cusa (1401-64): Cardinal, mathematician, scholar, experimental scientist, and influential philosopher who stressed the incomplete nature of humanity's knowledge of God and of the universe; Ptolemy (flourished 127-45, Alexandria

[Egypt]): Ancient astronomer, geographer, and mathematician who considered Earth the center of the universe (the "Ptolemaic system"). (Ed.)

16 See Erich Fromm, *Escape from Freedom* (1982), 70-71. (Turkish translation).

17 Pitirim A. Sorokin (1889-1968), Russian-American sociologist who was imprisoned three times by the czarist regime. After the October Revolution, he engaged in anti-Bolshevik activities. He emigrated to the US (1923), and gradually became a professor of sociology at the University of Minnesota (1924-30) and at Harvard (1930-55). His writings cover the breadth of sociology.

18 Odysseus: Hero of Homer's epic poem the *Odyssey* and one of the most frequently portrayed figures in Western literature.

19 Martin Luther (1483-46): German priest and scholar whose questioning of certain church practices led to the Protestant Reformation. He is one of the pivotal figures of Western civilization, as well as of Christianity; John Calvin (1509-64): The leading French Protestant Reformer and most important figure in the Protestant Reformation's second generation. The Calvinist form of Protestantism is widely thought to have had a major impact on the formation of the modern world. (Ed.)

20 M. Fethullah Gülen, *The Essentials of the Islamic Faith* (NJ: The Light, Inc., 2005), 249-50.

21 S. H. Nasr, *Man and Nature* (London: 1976), 94-95.

22 Said Nursi, "20th Word," *The Words*; Fethullah Gülen, *Essentials*, 275-79.

23 See "The second station of the Twentieth Word" in Said Nursi, *The Words* (NJ: The Light, Inc., 2005).

24 Jacques-Yves Cousteau (1910-97): French naval officer and ocean explorer, known for his extensive undersea investigations. (Ed.)

25 Muslim, *Fitan*, 110; Tirmidhi, *Fitan*, 59.

26 René Descartes (1596-1650): French mathematician, scientist, and philosopher; known as the "father of modern philosophy" because he was one of the first to oppose scholastic Aristotelianism. He began by methodically doubting knowledge based on authority, the senses, and reason, and then found certainty in the intuition that he exists when he is thinking. Thus his famous statement: "I think, therefore I am." (Ed.)

27 God uses angels and what we call material causes because Divinity's Dignity and Grandeur requires that people do not attribute directly to God that which they find disagreeable and accuse the Almighty thereof.

28 See "The Twenty-ninth Word, First Aim" in Said Nursi, *The Words* (NJ: The Light, Inc., 2005), pp. 526-7.

29 This was published in *American Scientist* (1995) and included in M. Fethullah Gülen, *The Essentials of the Islamic Faith* (NJ: The Light, Inc, 2005) p. 86.

30 Reported in *Discovery* (20 Aug. 1993).

31 Summarized from "The Fifteenth Word" in Said Nursi, *The Words* (NJ: The Light, Inc., 2005) pp. 193-206.

32 Unbelieving jinn and their human companions try to mislead people, especially through sorcery, mediumship, and soothsaying. (Ed.)

33 Morrison, *Man Does Not Stand Alone*, 100.

[34] Qur'anic commentators do not identify this person precisely. The majority of them think that he might have been a Prophet or a God-conscious king whom God equipped with great facilities so that he could realize great conquests. (Ed.)

[35] M. Bartusiac, "Sounds of the Sun," *American Scientist* (Jan.-Feb. 1994): 61-68.

[36] Said Nursi, *Muhakemat* (Reasonings) (Istanbul: c.1910), 68-69.

[37] Quoted in A. Adivar, *Ilim ve Din* (Science and Religion) (Istanbul: 1980), 282, and translated into English by the author.

[38] Paul Renteln, *American Scientist* (Nov.-Dec., 1991): 508.

[39] Werner Karl Heisenberg (1901-76): German physicist and philosopher who discovered a way to formulate quantum mechanics in terms of matrices (1925). In 1927 he published his indeterminacy (or uncertainty) principle, upon which he built his philosophy and for which he is best known. (Ed.)

[40] Paul Renteln, *Groping in the Light* (1990), 11-17.

[41] Muhiy al-Din ibn al-'Arabi (1165-1240): The "greatest Sufi master." His doctrine of the Transcendental Unity of Existence, which most have mistaken for monism and pantheism, made him the target of polemics. He wrote many books, the most famous of which are *Fusus al-Hikam* and *Al-Futuhat al-Makiyya*. (Ed.)

[42] Morrison, *Man Does Not Stand Alone*, 98-99.

[43] The Ahl al-Sunna wa al-Jama'a, meaning the People of Sunna and Community, are the great majority of Muslims who follow the way of the Prophet and the Companions. Other groups of Muslims, which can be called factions, differ from them with respect to either matters of belief (e.g., the Mu'tazila and Jabariya) or viewing the Companions' role in religion (e.g., the Kharijites and Shi'ah) because of political inclinations and influences from ancient philosophies. (Ed.)

[44] The Maturidi School: Followers of Abu Mansur Muhammad al-Maturidi (d. 944), who used logical arguments to defend orthodox Muslim theology. This school eventually became one of the two schools of Ahl al-Sunna wa al-Jama'a, the second being the Ash'ari School. (Ed.)

[45] The Ash'ari School: Followers of Abu al-Hasan al-Ash'ari (873/74-935/36), a Muslim Arab theologian noted for having integrated the rationalist methodology of the speculative theologians into the framework of orthodox Islam. (Ed.)

[46] M. S. Aksoy, "Artificial Intelligence: A Different Approach," *The Fountain*, no. 4 (Oct.-Dec. 1993): 10.

[47] Sir Roger Penrose (1931-): British mathematician [at Oxford] and relativist who in the 1960s calculated many basic features of black holes. (Ed.)

[48] Kurt Gödel (1906-78): Austrian-born U.S. mathematician, logician, and author of Gödel's proof, which states that within any rigidly logical mathematical system there are propositions (or questions) that cannot be proved or disproved on the basis of the axioms within that system and that, therefore, it is uncertain that the basic axioms of arithmetic will not give rise to contradictions. This proof has become a hallmark of 20th-century mathematics, and its repercussions continue to be felt and debated. (Ed.)

[49] Aksoy, "Artificial Intelligence," 11.

[50] Irfan Yilmaz, "Perfection and Primitiveness," *The Fountain*, no. 19 (July-Sept. 1997): 34-36.

CHAPTER 3
HUMANITY BETWEEN THE FALL
AND THE ASCENSION

1   Ibn Sina (980-1037): Iranian physician, the most famous and influential philoso-
    pher–scientist of Islam. He was particularly noted for his contributions in the fields
    of Aristotelian philosophy and medicine. (Ed.)

2   Translated by E. G. Browne, *A Literary History of Persia* and quoted by S. H. Nasr in
    Science and Civilization in Islam (London: 1987), 398-99.

3   They exist because there is One Who exists eternally and makes them exist; they have
    relative powers of seeing and hearing because there is One Who sees and hears
    absolutely and makes them see and hear; they have relative powers of acting and
    speaking because there is One Who never rests, sleeps, or dozes, and One Who has
    the absolute power of speech; they may have certain knowledge because there is One
    Who is the All-Knowing and enables them to learn; and they have relative power to
    do some things because there is One Who is the All-Powerful and gives them power.

4   What we mean by Christianity here is the form it assumed during the Middle Ages
    and which was represented mainly by the Catholic Church of that era. (Ed.)

5   Aldous Huxley (1894-1963): English novelist and critic gifted with an acute and far-
    ranging intelligence. His works were notable for their elegance, wit, and pessimistic
    satire. Huxley's deep distrust of 20th-century trends in both politics and technology
    found expression in *Brave New World* (1932), a nightmarish vision of a future socie-
    ty in which psychological conditioning forms the basis for a scientifically determined
    and immutable caste system. (Ed.)

6   Alexis Carrel, *Man: This Unknown* (Istanbul: 1983). Quoted and translated from its
    Turkish translation by R. Özdek.

7   Faust: Hero of one of the most durable legends in Western folklore and literature,
    the story of a German necromancer or astrologer who sells his soul to the devil in
    exchange for knowledge and power. (Ed.)

8   Sir Muhammad Iqbal (1877-1938) described the natural sciences as a flock of vul-
    tures, crowding round the flesh of nature and after each picking a part of it, flying
    off. This great Indian poet and philosopher was known for his influential efforts to
    establish Pakistan. (Ed.)

9   Erich Fromm, *Escape from Freedom*. Turkish translation by A. Yörükan, (Istanbul:
    1982); *Psychoanalysis and Religion*. Turkish translation by A. Aritan, (Istanbul: 1981).

10 See "The Twentieth Letter" in Said Nursi, *The Letters* (Turkey: The Light, Inc., 2002).

11 Max Scheler (1874-1928): German social and ethical philosopher remembered for
    his phenomenological approach based on the philosophical method of Edmund
    Husserl, the founder of phenomenology. As a phenomenologist, Scheler sought to
    discover the essence of mental attitudes and their relation to their objects. (Ed.)

12 This section was summarized from *Kant ve Scheler'de İnsan Problemi* (Humanity
    According to Kant and Scheler), (Istanbul: n.d.).

13 Quoted verbatim from Said Nursi, *The Words*, vol. 2 (Turkey: The Light, Inc., 2002).
    See the Twenty-third Word's Second Station.

CHAPTER 4
HOW WESTERN PHILOSOPHIES AND
THE QUR'AN VIEW HISTORY

1   Thomas Robert Malthus (1766-1834): English economist and demographer, best
    known for his theory that population growth will always tend to outrun the food
    supply and that humanity's betterment is impossible without stern limits on repro-
    duction. (Ed.)

2   Charles Darwin (1809-82): English naturalist renowned for his claim of evolution
    and his theory of its operation (Darwinism). His evolutionary theories, propounded
    chiefly in two works—*On the Origin of Species by Means of Natural Selection* (1859)
    and *The Descent of Man, and Selection in Relation to Sex* (1871)—have had a profound
    influence on subsequent scientific thought. (Ed.) [120] Maurice Bucaille, *What Is the
    Origin of Man?* Turkish trans. by A. Ünal, (Istanbul: 1984), 48-50.

3   Abdul-Hamid Siddiqi, *Tarihin Yorumu* (The Interpretation of History) (Istanbul:
    1978), 51.

4   Karl R. Popper, *The Poverty of Historicism* (London: 1976).

5   Nikolay Yakovlevich Danilevsky (1822-65): Russian naturalist and historical philoso-
    pher who was the first to propound the philosophy of history as a series of distinct
    civilizations and urged Russia to ignore Europe. (Ed.)

6   Arnold (Joseph) Toynbee (1889-1975): English historian whose 12-volume *A Study
    of History* (1934–61) put forward a much-discussed philosophy of history based on
    an analysis of the cyclical development and decline of civilizations. (Ed.)

7   Ibn Khaldun (1322-1406): The greatest Arab historian, who developed one of the ear-
    liest non-religious philosophies of history, contained in his masterpiece the *Muqaddima*
    (Introduction to History). (Ed.)

INDEX